Skylines and Other Dominance-Based Queries

Synthesis Lectures on Data Management

Editor
H.V. Jagadish, *University of Michigan*

Founding Editor
M. Tamer Özsu, *University of Waterloo*

Synthesis Lectures on Data Management is edited by H.V. Jagadish of the University of Michigan. The series publishes 80–150 page publications on topics pertaining to data management. Topics include query languages, database system architectures, transaction management, data warehousing, XML and databases, data stream systems, wide scale data distribution, multimedia data management, data mining, and related subjects.

Skylines and Other Dominance-Based Queries
Apostolos N. Papadopoulos, Eleftherios Tiakas, Theodoros Tzouramanis, Nikolaos Georgiadis, and Yannis Manolopoulos
2020

Cloud-Based RDF Data Management
Zoi Kaoudi, Ioana Manolescu, and Stamatis Zampetakis
2020

Community Search over Big Graphs
Xin Huang, Laks V.S. Lakshmanan, and Jianliang Xu
2019

On Transactional Concurrency Control
Goetz Graefe
2019

Data-Intensive Workflow Management: For Clouds and Data-Intensive and Scalable Computing Environments
Daniel C.M. de Oliveira, Ji Liu, and Esther Pacitti
2019

Answering Queries Using Views, Second Edition
Foto Afrati and Rada Chirkova
2019

Skylines and Other Dominance-Based Queries

Apostolos N. Papadopoulos, Eleftherios Tiakas, Theodoros Tzouramanis, Nikolaos Georgiadis, and Yannis Manolopoulos

ISBN: 978-3-031-00748-4   paperback
ISBN: 978-3-031-01876-3   ebook
ISBN: 978-3-031-00103-1   hardcover

DOI 10.1007/978-3-031-01876-3

A Publication in the Springer series
SYNTHESIS LECTURES ON DATA MANAGEMENT

Lecture #63
Series Editor: H.V. Jagadish, *University of Michigan*
Founding Editor: M. Tamer Özsu, *University of Waterloo*
Series ISSN
Print 2153-5418   Electronic 2153-5426

Skylines and Other Dominance-Based Queries

Apostolos N. Papadopoulos
School of Informatics, Aristotle University of Thessaloniki, Greece

Eleftherios Tiakas
School of Informatics, Aristotle University of Thessaloniki, Greece

Theodoros Tzouramanis
Department of Computer Science & Biomedical Informatics, University of Thessaly, Greece

Nikolaos Georgiadis
School of Informatics, Aristotle University of Thessaloniki, Greece

Yannis Manolopoulos
School of Pure & Applied Sciences, Open University of Cyprus, Cyprus

SYNTHESIS LECTURES ON DATA MANAGEMENT #63

ABSTRACT

This book is a gentle introduction to dominance-based query processing techniques and their applications. The book aims to present fundamental as well as some advanced issues in the area in a precise, but easy-to-follow, manner. Dominance is an intuitive concept that can be used in many different ways in diverse application domains. The concept of dominance is based on the values of the attributes of each object. An object p dominates another object q if p is *better* than q. This goodness criterion may differ from one user to another. However, all decisions boil down to the minimization or maximization of attribute values. In this book, we will explore algorithms and applications related to dominance-based query processing. The concept of dominance has a long history in finance and multi-criteria optimization. However, the introduction of the concept to the database community in 2001 inspired many researchers to contribute to the area. Therefore, many algorithmic techniques have been proposed for the efficient processing of dominance-based queries, such as skyline queries, k-dominant queries, and top-k dominating queries, just to name a few.

KEYWORDS

multi-dimensional data, preference-based queries, dominance, skyline queries, range skylines, skyline cubes, top-k dominating queries, k-dominance, dynamic skylines, spatial skylines, metric-based dominance queries, multi-criteria decision-making, applications

To our families

Contents

List of Figures

List of Tables

Preface

The main objective of this book is to provide an easy-to-follow, self-contained, and concise coverage of dominance-based query-processing techniques. During the last two decades a large corpus of relevant research results has been accumulated. For instance, if someone searches in a digital library, such as Digital Bibliography & Library Project (DBLP), she will realize that more than 1,000 of papers have been published in scientific journals and conference proceedings, besides to technical reports and theses.

It turns out that dominance-based queries have many interesting applications in diverse scientific fields. Therefore, the book may be followed easily by non-computer science students. For example, the application of dominance in finance, healthcare, Internet of Things, scientometrics, and many other fields makes this book relevant to a broader audience.

Most of this book does not require specialized background. However, the content is better suited for students and practitioners that have basic knowledge of data structures and database systems. More specifically, the target audience includes:

- graduate students who want to enhance their knowledge in more advanced query processing techniques. The material of the book may be part of a data management-oriented course;

- M.Sc. students who wish to better understand the concept and the applications of dominance-based query processing;

- Ph.D. students and researchers who wish to master the most important concepts in dominance-based query processing and may want to apply these ideas in more complex problems that involve user preferences; and

- practitioners who wish to learn about dominance-based queries and apply these ideas in data management and mining tasks in the field of their expertise.

We really hope that this book will be a valuable companion toward understanding the concepts and techniques related to dominance-based query processing. The interested reader can focus further on the selected bibliography. It is certain that the research community will devote more human and financial resources in the area in the years to come.

Apostolos N. Papadopoulos, Eleftherios Tiakas, Theodoros Tzouramanis, Nikolaos Georgiadis, and Yannis Manolopoulos
November 2020

Acknowledgments

The authors would like to thank Professors Hosagrahar Visvesvaraya Jagadish and Tamer Özsu for accepting our book in the *Syntesis Lectures in Data Management* series. Also, we are grateful to Diane Cerra and Christine Kiilerich for their great assistance during the preparation of the book. Moreover, the authors would like to acknowledge the assistance of collaborators and friends who were involved in research works cited in this book. More specifically, the authors are grateful to: Dimitrios Gunopulos, Dimitrios Katsaros, Maria Kontaki, Alexandros Nanopoulos, Timos Sellis, Yannis Theodoridis, and Georgios Valkanas.

Apostolos N. Papadopoulos, Eleftherios Tiakas, Theodoros Tzouramanis, Nikolaos Georgiadis, and Yannis Manolopoulos
November 2020

CHAPTER 1

Introduction

This chapter introduces some important concepts related to dominance-based query processing. It presents some key terms and a brief history of the concept of dominance. Although the book assumes a Database perspective to the concept of dominance, we will see that the first research works appeared in other disciplines such as Computational Geometry, Multi-Objective Optimization, and Economics.

1.1 OBJECTS AND ATTRIBUTES

In real-life applications, entities are usually modeled as *objects* that are associated with *attributes*. For example, a laptop computer may be described by attributes like *weight*, *price*, and *screen size*, just to name a few. As another example, a hotel may contain attributes like *price* and *distance from the beach*.

As long as we focus on one attribute only, it is very easy to decide if laptop l_1 is better than laptop l_2, or if hotel h_1 is better than hotel h_2. For example, if we focus on the price attribute, then cheaper is better and, therefore, the best laptop is the one with the minimum price (all other factors being equal). Alas, if we focus on price alone, soon we will realize that the cheapest laptop has only 4 GB of main memory and it weighs 5 kg! But this is natural, since the only goodness criterion we specified is the price of the item. Similar arguments hold for the hotel example, i.e., the cheapest hotel may be located 5 km from the beach, which is not ideal for vacations and sea sports. On the other hand, a hotel that is located very close to the beach is expected to be more expensive. From these simple examples we deduce that the more attributes we take into account, the harder to determine the *best* items to choose.

For the rest of this book, we will assume that objects are represented as *points* in a multi-dimensional space, where the number of dimensions equals the number of attributes. Moreover, in general, we will assume that all attributes assume numerical values (e.g., integers or floats). Therefore, an object is represented by a point $p = (p \cdot x_1, p \cdot x_2, \ldots, p \cdot x_d) \in \mathbb{R}^d$, where d is the number of dimensions and x_i denotes the value of the ith dimension. However, in real-life applications, attributes may be *categorical*. We will handle categorical attributes differently when needed.

Depending on the application domain, the total number of attributes associated with the objects under consideration may be low or very high. In low-dimensional spaces problem solving is usually easier in comparison to high-dimensional spaces. For example, in the two-dimensional space many Computational Geometry problems are solvable in $\mathcal{O}(n \log n)$, whereas for higher dimensions the complexity is higher and in many cases increases exponentially with respect to d, number of dimensions (the curse of dimensionality). However, even if the total number of dimensions is high, a user may focus on a small subset of the available dimensions. For example, even if a laptop has a significant number of attributes, a specific user may be interested in *price* and *memory* only, which means that laptops may be represented in the two-dimensional space.

The most straightforward approach for attacking the problem is to map multi-dimensional objects to a single value by using a user-defined *ranking function* (also known as *scoring function*). The value of this function defines the *goodness* of the corresponding object. In its simplest form, the ranking function takes into account all or some of the attributes and computes an output value in the range [0, 1]. A natural assumption is that values close to one denote *good* objects, whereas values close to zero denote low-ranked items.

It is natural to assume that the ranking function is monotone with respect to the values of the attributes. This means that when the value of an attribute becomes better, the score of the object is increased. A simple example of a ranking function is the sum of the attribute values. In most of the cases, a weighted sum is being used, since summing values from different attributes may result in bias. Formally, a weighted-sum ranking function $F(p) \in [0, 1]$ may have the following form:

$$F(p) = \sum_{i=1}^{d} w_i \cdot p \cdot x_i.$$

Given a specific ranking function, a baseline algorithm to detect the k best objects is to apply the function to all points and then to select the k with the highest score. In general, the process of selecting the best k objects is referred to as a top-k query and in practice more efficient algorithms are being used instead of the baseline (Ilyas et al., 2008). The great advantage of top-k queries is that once the monotone ranking function $F()$ has been decided all objects are mapped in the one-dimensional space where detecting the best k is intuitive. The challenge in top-k processing, however, is to provide efficient algorithmic techniques in order to avoid the score computation of all objects (Fagin, 1996). Evidently, this is also related to the specific ranking function being used.

In many cases a ranking function cannot be easily defined, depending on the attribute types of the objects and the number of them. Moreover, since usually the ranking function is user-defined, different functions lead to different results. The question we are going to answer in the sequel is "what one can do if a ranking function is not available?"

1.2   THE CONCEPT OF DOMINANCE

Preference-based queries are considered important because they take into account user's constraints which are expressed by either a *ranking function*, or by specifying if the attributes of the objects in the result should be *maximized* (be as high as possible) or *minimized* (be as small as possible). This book focuses on the second category of algorithmic techniques that they do not require an explicit user-defined ranking function and instead they use the concept of *dominance* to provide an intuitive way for ranking.

Dominance refers to a situation where an object p is better than another object q. In our case, objects are represented as multi-dimensional points. We will assume, without loss of generality, that in each dimension small values are preferable. Note that even if in some cases larger values are preferable, we may convert the problem to an equivalent one such that smaller values are preferable (e.g., by subtracting the values from the maximum).

Definition 1.1 (dominance). An object $p = (p \cdot x_1, p \cdot x_2, \ldots, p \cdot x_d) \in \mathbb{R}^d$ dominates another object $q = (q \cdot x_1, q \cdot x_2, \ldots, q \cdot x_d) \in \mathbb{R}^d$, i.e., $p \prec q$, when: $\forall i \in \{1, \ldots, d\} : p \cdot x_i \leq q \cdot x_i \wedge \exists i \in \{1, \ldots, d\} : p \cdot x_i < q \cdot x_i$. This means that p is as good as q in all dimensions, and it is strictly better than q in at least one dimension.

It is not hard to prove that the dominance relationship is transitive, which means that if $p \prec q$ and $q \prec r$ then $p \prec r$. Let us present some examples demonstrating the dominance relationship. The point $p = (1, 3)$ dominates the point $q = (3, 4)$ since p is strictly better in all dimensions. Also, the point $p = (1, 2, 3)$ dominates the point $q = (1, 2, 4)$ since although both points have the same values in the first two dimensions, p is strictly better than q in the third dimension. Finally, $p = (1, 2, 3, 4)$ does not dominate $q = (1, 2, 3, 4)$ (and vice versa) since both points have the same values in all dimensions and therefore the conditions of Definition 1.1 are not satisfied.

Given two points p and q we identify three different cases related to dominance:

- p dominates q $(p \prec q)$,

- q dominates p $(q \prec p)$, and

- p and q are equivalent $(p \simeq q)$.

Essentially, p and q are equivalent when the following conditions hold: $p \nprec q$ and $q \nprec p$, i.e., no point dominates over the other. Assume that $p = (1, 10)$ and $q = (2, 5)$. In this case, although p is better in the first dimension, q is better in the second dimension. There is no clear winner between p and q in this case, which again means that $p \simeq q$.

Figure 1.1 presents a set of points in the two-dimensional space. In Figure 1.1a we observe that $p \prec r, r \prec t, p \prec t, q \prec r, q \prec s, q \prec t, s \prec t$. In addition, we observe that $p \simeq q, p \simeq s$, $r \simeq s$. With any point p there is an associated *dominance region* $DR(p)$ which contains all points of the universe dominated by p. For example, in Figure 1.1b, the dominance region of q is painted yellow. Any point enclosed by the yellow region is dominated by q. Simply stated, a point p is better than all points contained in $DR(p)$, which means that the attribute values of p are at least as good as those of any point $q \in DR(p)$.

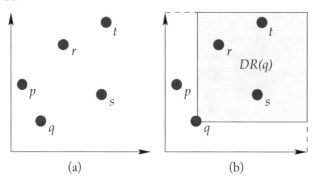

Figure 1.1: The concept of dominance.

Definition 1.2   (dominance region).   The dominance region of a point $p = (p \cdot x_1, p \cdot x_2, \ldots, p \cdot x_d) \in \mathbb{R}^d$ is defined as the set of points $DR(p)$ such that for any point $q \in DR(p)$ it holds that $p \prec q$.

1.3   BEST POINTS

Given a set of points P and the dominance relationship between points in P, an interesting question to answer is "which are the best points?" Perhaps the simplest approach is to define goodness based on dominance, by assuming that a point is considered "one of the best" if it is *not dominated*. This concept was first discussed by Vilfredo Pareto, an Italian engineer, sociologist, economist, political scientist, and philosopher.[1] In fact, finding the best points is considered an optimization problem. In many cases instead of a set of points, we are given a set of inequalities or functions that must be minimized or maximized. As mentioned previously, without loss of generality, we will assume that smaller values are preferable.

Assume that objects are represented as points in the two-dimensional space, where the attributes are x_1 and x_2. Assume further that the user defines two linear functions $g()$ and $f()$ as follows: $g(x_1, x_2) = 2x_1 + x_2$, $f(x_1, x_2) = x_1 + 3x_2$. These two functions along with some interesting points are illustrated in Figure 1.2a. An interesting problem appears when we try to optimize at the same time both functions. Without loss of generality, we assume that we want to minimize the functions $g()$ and $f()$ (for example, imagine that $g()$ corresponds to the cost and $f()$ corresponds to the time required to produce a specific item). It is meaningful to assume that the best solution is the one that minimizes both the cost (function $g()$) and the required production time (function $f()$).

Table 1.1 presents the attribute values for points a, b, c, d, and e of Figure 1.2a. The table presents both the coordinates of every point in the original space (design space) and the

[1]https://en.wikipedia.org/wiki/Vilfredo_Pareto

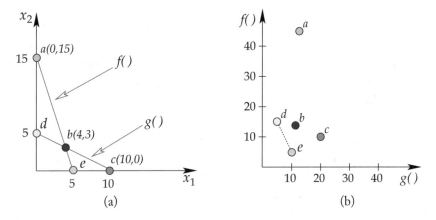

Figure 1.2: Design space (a) and criterion space (b).

Table 1.1: Interesting points in original (design) space and transformed (criterion) space

Point	x_1	x_2	$g(x_1, x_2)$	$f(x_1, x_2)$
a	0	15	15	45
b	4	3	11	13
c	10	0	20	10
d	0	5	5	15
e	5	0	10	5

coordinates in the criterion space, i.e., when the coordinates of every point correspond to the values of the functions $g()$ and $f()$ that we want to minimize. By using the functions $g()$ and $f()$, all points are transformed to the criterion space, depicted in Figure 1.2b. It is not hard to verify that point d minimizes the function $g()$, whereas point e minimizes the function $f()$. The rows corresponding to these points are highlighted in Table 1.1. The question we need to answer is which points (if any) are the ones that minimize both $g()$ and $f()$. It turns out that the best answers are located on the straight line connecting points d and e, as shown in Figure 1.2b. This line is known as the *Pareto front*. Any point located on the line connecting d and e is considered as *Pareto optimal*. By a closer look at Figure 1.2b we observe that points d and e are not dominated. The same holds for all points located on the straight line connecting d and e. Similar arguments can be expressed if more than two functions are used.

By inspecting Figure 1.2b as well as Table 1.1, it is evident that points d and e have a special role: they are not dominated. This means that all other points are dominated by at least one point. For example, $b \prec a$, $d \prec a$, $e \prec a$, $e \prec b$, $e \prec c$. Based on the previous discussion, points d and e (and all points lying on the line segment (d,e)) are considered the best.

Definition 1.3 (minima).   Given a set of multi-dimensional points P, there is a unique subset $S \subseteq P$ which contains the points from P that are not dominated by any other point. The members of S are also known as the *minima* of the set P.

In some cases, instead of referring to *minima* we refer to *maxima*. The two terms are equivalent, since the first is related to the *minimization* of the attribute values, whereas the second is related to the *maximization* of the attributed values. As we have mentioned previously, these cases are symmetric and are considered equivalent since there is no essential difference in the algorithms that process either version of the problem. The problem of finding the minima/maxima of a set of points has a long history in diverse disciplines. It has been used in Computational Geometry (Kung et al., 1975; Preparata and Shamos, 1985) and in general in Multi-Objective Optimization (Das and Dennis, 1998; Lin, 1976). However, there was a burst of dominance-based algorithmic techniques after the introduction of the topic to the Database community by Börzsönyi et al. (2001). In the Database community the minima of a set of points P is known as the *skyline* of P.

Definition 1.4 (skyline query).   Given a potentially large collection of points P in the d-dimensional space, the skyline query returns a subset of P, written as $SKY(P)$, containing the points that are not dominated. More formally: $\forall s \in SKY(P), \nexists q \in P : q \prec s$.

The skyline query was the first dominance-based query studied by the database community and many algorithms have been proposed under different settings. For example, some algorithms assume the existence of an index, whereas some others assume that such an index does not exist. Also, some algorithms assume that the data fit in main memory, whereas some others do not make such an assumption. Moreover, we will several algorithms have been proposed to work in a parallel/distributed environment, where multiple processors and/or disks are available. Many of these topics are covered in the subsequent chapters.

The literature is very rich in research works related to the topic of dominance-based query processing. Here, we just mention some interesting survey papers that the reader may study to get a broad view of the area. A gentle introduction to skyline queries may be found in Thakur (2017). Also, a short survey of the topic is reported in Tiakas et al. (2015). A more thorough and technical coverage of the skyline topic may be found in Chomicki et al. (2013). A extensive survey of skyline queries is reported in Kalyvas and Tzouramanis (2017). Finally, Hose and Vlachou (2011) discusses in detail skyline processing in distributed systems. More reading resources will be provided for the topics covered in the following chapters.

1.4   BOOK ROADMAP

This book is about dominance-based queries, i.e., preference queries that use the dominance relationship between objects, which are represented as multi-dimensional points. After this gentle introduction, we are ready to dive deeper into the concept and investigate algorithmic techniques related to dominance-based query processing. The rest of the book is organized as follows.

The next chapter, Chapter 2, focuses on the processing of skyline queries under different settings, such as in main memory, in secondary memory, index-free, index-based. Both index-free and index-based techniques are important based on the way processing is being performed. Next, Chapter 3 discusses some significant variations of the skyline problem that have been studied in the literature. These variations are based on simple modifications to the original problem, that may change drastically the output. One of these variations, the top-k dominating query, has attracted significant research interest. For this reason, we devote Chapter 4 to the study of top-k dominating queries under different settings. Finally, Chapter 5 discusses interesting applications of the dominance concept in diverse fields, such as image retrieval and network analysis.

1.5   SUMMARY

Dominance-based queries are preference queries that use the concept of dominance between the objects. Objects are accompanied by several attribute values and therefore it is natural to assume that objects may be represented as points in a multi-dimensional feature space with d dimensions. Depending on the application, d may be small (e.g., 2, 3, 5) or large (e.g., 10, 20, or larger).

Between two points p and q we may define a dominance relationship where p dominates q if p is at least as *good* as q in all dimensions and it is strictly *better* than q in at least one dimension. From the previous sentence it is evident that dominance is based on a goodness criterion, which depends on the attribute under consideration and the preference of the user. For example, some users prefer a laptop with a large screen, whereas for others a small screen is preferable. Without loss of generality, we assume that always *smaller values are preferable*, i.e., we aim to minimize attribute values.

Given a set of points P a user may be interested in the *best* points. The only information required by the system should be the minimization or maximization of attribute values. The system should report back to the user a set of points that satisfy the goodness criteria and they are not dominated by any other point. This set of the best points is known as the skyline of P. This problem had been studied before under different perspectives in Multi-Objective Optimization and Computational Geometry. In this book, we take a Database perspective and we cover algorithmic techniques for skyline query processing as well as for processing variations and extensions of the original problem.

CHAPTER 2

Skyline Queries

This chapter focuses on skyline query processing algorithms. First, we discuss algorithms that return the skyline of a set of points P that can fit in main memory. Next, we present techniques that are based on secondary memory. We cover both index-free and index-based query processing algorithms and we discuss about their advantages and disadvantages.

2.1 MAIN-MEMORY COMPUTATION

In this section, we discuss some simple algorithmic techniques to answer a skyline query when the point set P can be accommodated in main-memory. This means that the set of points P may be stored in an array of size n, where $n = |P|$. In fact, this is an ideal situation, since the processing cost in this case is dominated by the CPU time. Later, we will relax the assumption that P fits in main-memory and investigate what happens when P is too large to fit in the main memory.

In every problem, there is a brute-force (i.e., baseline) algorithm that solves it, which is simple but (usually) very inefficient with respect to complexity. The brute-force algorithm (termed BF) for the skyline problem works in a very intuitive way, by checking all possible pairs of points (p, q) and testing if $p \prec q$. In such a case, q is eliminated since it cannot be part of the skyline result (it is dominated by at least another point). On the other hand, all points that survive are returned as the skyline result ($SKY(P)$). Evidently, to avoid checking a pair of points twice, we prioritize points based on their identifier. Therefore, with each point $p \in P$ we associate an integer $id(p)$ which is the unique identifier of p.

The steps required by the BF algorithm are shown in Algorithm 2.1. The algorithm receives as input the set of points P and returns the set $SKY(P)$. Observe the nested loop that generates all possible pairs of points of P. When a point is dominated at least once, it is excluded from the result (Line 5). When the nested loop terminates, the set $SKY(P)$ contains all points that are not dominated. This set is returned back to the user.

Note that the BF algorithm works for any number of dimensions, the only requirement being that the set P must fit in main memory. The number of dimensions (d) has an impact only on the cost of the dominance check performed in Line 4. However, there is a significant disadvantage: the BF algorithm requires quadratic complexity! The nested loop forces the algorithm to perform $\mathcal{O}(n^2)$ dominance checks, where n is the number of points in P. In addition, each dominance check requires $\mathcal{O}(d)$ comparisons, where d is the number of dimensions. Therefore, the baseline algorithm in d dimensions requires $\mathcal{O}(dn^2)$ primitive operations.

Algorithm 2.1 Brute-force Skyline Computation (BF)

Input : set of points P
Output : the skyline of P ($SKY(P)$)

1: $SKY(P) \leftarrow P$ /* *initially all points are skyline points* */
2: **for all** $p \in P$ **do**
3:     **for all** $q \in SKY(P), id(q) > id(p)$ **do**
4:         **if** $p \prec q$ **then**
5:             $SKY(P) \leftarrow SKY(P) - \{q\}$ /* *remove q from the skyline result* */
6:         **end if**
7:     **end for**
8: **end for**
9: **return** $SKY(P)$

Figure 2.1: Skyline in one dimension ($d = 1$).

It is expected that for small cardinalities, the BF algorrithm will be quite efficient. However, as the number of points increases the performance of BF is expected to deteriorate fast, due to the quadratic complexity of the algorithm. Therefore, a more efficient algorithm is required to avoid the quadratic trap. By observing the BF algorithm, it is evident that there are many unnecessary dominance checks that are executed, since the order that the pairs of points are checked is totally random, lacking a principled approach.

To better understand this concept, assume for the time being that $d = 1$, i.e., points are essentially numbers in one dimension (objects have only one attribute). By assuming further that attribute values are unique (without loss of generality), it is not hard to show that the skyline of P consists of one point only, the one with the minimum attribute value. This is shown in Figure 2.1, where the only dimension present corresponds to the attribute *price*. Among the points (e.g., products), p is the only one that is not dominated and, therefore, it is the only member of the skyline result.

In such a case, running the BF algorithm results in a waste of resources since we just need to determine the minimum value from a set of numbers, which can be done in linear time ($\mathcal{O}(n)$) instead of $\mathcal{O}(n^2)$. This simple example demonstrates that perhaps we can solve the problem faster than the BF algorithm. This intuition is correct, as it is shown in the sequel.

The next step is to check what happens when $d = 2$, i.e., when the set P is composed of two-dimensional points. Again, we assume that P can be accommodated in main memory.

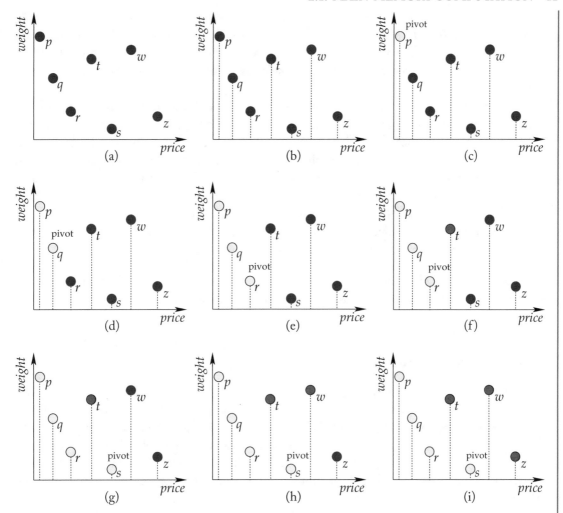

Figure 2.2: Skyline query processing for $d = 2$.

The set P is shown in Figure 2.2a. It seems that the existence of a second attribute increases the problem complexity. Our intuition says that we are expecting that more points in general will be part of the skyline. This intuition will be proven correct, since the dimensionality is one factor that affects the number of skyline points.

To attack the two-dimensional skyline problem by avoiding the quadratic trap, first let us sort the points in P in increasing order based on the x axis (i.e., the *price* attribute). The projections of all points on the x axis are shown in Figure 2.2b. The examination of points in P is based on the ascending x axis order, starting from the point with the minimum *price* value, which is point p. Since p has the minimum value of the *price* dimension, it is the first member of the skyline set *SKY*. To support this decision, it suffices to say that since p has the minimum *price* value, it is not possible that p is dominated by another point. Point p has a special role for the time being; it is the *pivot* point (or else, the *reference* point). The current situation is depicted in Figure 2.2c.

The next point to test is point q. Every subsequent point according to the set order is checked against the pivot point. Since point q is not dominated by the pivot point p, q is inserted in *SKY* and also q becomes a new pivot point as well. Currently, the skyline set is composed of points p and q, i.e., $SKY(P) = \{p, q\}$, as shown in Figure 2.2d. One may think that the decision to include q in the skyline set it is not sufficiently justified. In fact, q can be dominated only by a point met before q. However, the only point that we discovered before q is p, and as we have seen, p does not dominate q. On the other hand, q cannot be dominated by points following q, since q has a smaller *price* value than all subsequent points. Therefore, q can be safely included in the skyline set. This observation is expressed by the following lemma.

Lemma 2.1   *Let p and q be two consecutive points in the ascending order created by using the x coordinates (i.e., projections on the x axis). Then either $p \prec q$ or $p \simeq q$.*

Proof. Evidently, q cannot dominate p since the x value of q is larger that the x value of p. Therefore, depending on the y values of p and q, either $p \prec q$ or $p \simeq q$.   □

Note that we have assumed that all x coordinates are unique, i.e., there are no duplicates with respect to the x coordinate. However, even in the (more realistic) case where we may have ties in the x values, the lemma still holds by considering that from each group of points with the same x coordinate, we will select the one with the minimum y value. This may be easily achieved by enforcing a *lexicographic* order over all attributes instead of sorting based on the x coordinate alone, in order to first check points with small attribute values in case of ties on the other attributes.

Let us return to our running example. The next point to process is r. Note that the current pivot q does not dominate r. Therefore, r is inserted in the skyline set and becomes the new pivot, whereas the algorithm continues to examine the subsequent candidate point, which is point t. Since $r \prec t$, the pivot remains the same and the algorithm checks the next point which is s. Evidently, $r \simeq s$ and, therefore, s is inserted into the skyline set and becomes the next pivot. Finally, w and z are both dominated by s. Since there are no more points to check, the algorithm terminates and the final skyline set is $SKY(P) = \{p, q, r, s\}$.

The basic idea of the above process is shown in Algorithm 2.2. First, the algorithms sort all points according to the x coordinates (Line 2). Note that in case of ties (as mentioned previously) a lexicographic order is required instead of just using the x coordinates. Then, it checks all points in order. The first point, p_1, becomes the pivot and is inserted in $SKY(P)$ since it is the point with the minimum x coordinate, and therefore cannot be dominated. Then, every time the pivot

---

Algorithm 2.2 Sort-based (SB) Skyline Computation

_____*Input :* set of points P

Output : the skyline of P $(SKY(P))$ _____

1: $SKY(P) \leftarrow \emptyset$
2: sort P based on x coordinates /* *let p_i be the i th point in order* */
3: $i \leftarrow 1$
4: *pivot* = the point with the minimum x coordinate (p_1)
5: $SKY(P) \leftarrow SKY(P) \cup pivot$
6: $i \leftarrow i + 1$
7: **while** $i \leq n$ **do**
8:    **if** *pivot* $\simeq p_i$ **then**
9:       *pivot* $\leftarrow p_i$ /* *update the pivot point* */
10:       $SKY(P) \leftarrow SKY(P) \cup p_i$ /* *update the skyline result* */
11:    **end if**
12:    $i \leftarrow i + 1$
13: **end while**
14: **return** $SKY(P)$

---

does not dominate a subsequent point p_i, then p_i is inserted in $SKY(P)$ and becomes the new pivot. If p_i is dominated by the pivot then p_i is simply discarded and the pivot remains the same. This process is followed until all points are examined.

It is not hard to verify that the worst-case complexity of the previous algorithm is $\mathcal{O}(n \log n)$, due to the sorting operation in Line 2. However, it turns out that the same worst-case complexity is achieved for $d = 3$, i.e., in the three-dimensional space, as was shown in Kung et al. (1975). For higher dimensionalities, i.e., $d \geq 4$ the worst-case bound according to Kung et al. (1975) is $\mathcal{O}(n(\log n)^{d-2})$. The bound shows clearly the dependency on both the number of points (n) in P and the space dimensionality (d). Later in this chapter, we will show that the data distribution plays a very important role not only for the cost of the skyline computation but for the skyline cardinality as well (i.e., the number of points contained in $SKY(P)$).

2.2   ALGORITHMS FOR SECONDARY MEMORY

Although skyline computation in main memory is important and very useful, there are cases where we need to resort to secondary storage. In fact, taking into account the size of the datasets used by modern applications, it is natural to assume that the dataset cannot be accommodated in main memory. Therefore, algorithmic techniques for skyline computation are required that will work with disk-resident data.

There are two different lines of algorithmic techniques than one may follow that use different query processing algorithms. Both directions have their own arguments as presented below.

- The first direction does not depend on specific indexing techniques. For example, there are many datasets collected and archived without indexing. Moreover, if the skyline query is executed on top of the result of another query, it is very unlikely that an index will be available. Also, if an index exists that manages all d dimensions, asking for the skyline in a subset of the available dimensions renders the index inapplicable.

- The second direction involves techniques that are based on a specific indexing mechanism for multi-dimensional points. Indeed, in many cases an index is available and therefore it can be used to speed-up skyline computation. For example, if the skyline query processing algorithm is implemented inside a database management system, then an index (e.g., an R-tree as in Guttman (1984)) may be available and it may be used toward an improved query processing performance.

2.2.1   INDEX-FREE TECHNIQUES

Index-free techniques do not rely on the existence of an index for the point set P. Thus, it is expected that their cost will be higher than that of index-based techniques.

Block-Nested Loop (BNL)

A naive algorithm to compute a skyline query is to compare every object with every other object of the dataset by using a nested loop. However, the quadratic complexity $\mathcal{O}(n^2)$ makes this algorithm very inefficient (where n is the total number of points in P).

The Block-Nested Loop (BNL) algorithm according to Börzsönyi et al. (2001) applies the same idea, but uses a window (memory blocks with limited space) that holds a limited number of data objects. BNL applies multiple iterations until the final result is formed. The basic steps of the algorithm are as follows.

- Each candidate object p is checked if it is dominated by any other object from the window.

- If this happens, then p is eliminated.

- If p dominates some objects from the window, then these objects are eliminated, and p is inserted into the window.

- Finally, if p is incomparable (i.e., equivalent) with all objects in the window, then it is inserted into the window.

In case the window is full, a temporary disk file is used to hold the candidate objects. This file will be checked in the next iteration, since it contains objects that were not eliminated in the previous iteration. At the end of each iteration, all objects from the window that have been compared to all objects contained in the temporary file may be written to the skyline result since they are not dominated. To keep track of the comparisons that must be performed, the concept of *timestamp* is being used. Each object p of the window receives a timestamp $TS(p)$ that records the time that p was inserted into the window. Also, each object q of the temporary file receives a timestamp $TS'(q)$ that records the time q was inserted in the temporary file. If the next object that we read from the temporary file is q, then all objects p from the window with $TS(p) < TS'(q)$ are part of the skyline result.

The BNL algorithm works well when the skyline result is relatively small; it requires a predefined limited memory size (the window). The worst-case complexity with respect to the number of dominance remains $\mathcal{O}(n^2)$, however, with a much better I/O behavior in practice. In addition, variants of BNL have been proposed in Börzsönyi et al. (2001), by maintaining the window as a self-organized list and by replacing objects in the window to keep the most dominant set. Taking into account that we are working in d dimensions, each dominance check costs $\mathcal{O}(d)$ primitive operations. Therefore, the worst-case complexity of BNL with respect to the number of primitive operations is $\mathcal{O}(dn^2)$.

Sort Filter Skyline (SFS)

A very efficient variation of BNL is the Sort-Filter-Skyline algorithm (SFS) proposed in Chomicki et al. (2005), which is based on presorting the points based on a monotone function, which is equivalent to a topological ordering. The presorting step of SFS makes the query processing efficient and well behaved in a relational setting. Below, we highlight the most important characteristics of the SFS algorithm.

Let W denote the window being used to accommodate points that are not dominated. It turns out that for SFS, the set W is always a subset of $SKY(P)$, i.e., it contains only skyline points. This means that if a point enters W it will never be deleted since it is guaranteed to be a skyline point. This feature of SFS suggests that it is impossible for a point in W to be dominated by a point found later in the ordering. Let $f()$ be a monotone function based on the coordinates of the points. For example, $f(p)$ may be defined as the sum of coordinates of point p. Let also p_i be the ith point based on the sorted order. The topological order guarantees that for two points p_i and p_j, if $j > i$ (i.e., p_i is located before p_j in the sorted order) then $p_j \nprec p_i$, which means that p_j cannot dominate p_i. Therefore, either $p_i \prec p_j$ or $p_i \simeq p_j$. In case where p_j is not dominated by any point in W, then p_j is inserted into W and it is marked as a skyline point.

The pseudocode of SFS is given in Algorithm 2.3. Note that the algorithm is very similar to the sort-based (SB) technique shown in Algorithm 2.2. The main differences are that SFS handles points in secondary memory and also a different monotone function is being used for sorting. Moreover, SFS works for any number of dimensions, whereas SB can be applied only for $d = 2$. In the pseudocode we highlight Line 2 (sorting) as well as Line 7 which checks if the next point in the topological order (p_i) is dominated by any point currently stored in the window ($SKY(P)$).

Based on Chomicki et al. (2005), a monotone function $f()$ based on *entropy* showed the best performance with respect to the number of dominance checks. If $p[j]$ denotes the value of the jth dimension (attribute) of point p, then the order of the points in P is performed by the following entropy-based monotone function:

$$f(p) = \sum_{j=1}^{d} \ln(p[j] + 1). \qquad (2.1)$$

SFS Optimizations (LESS and SaLSa)

Although SFS shows significant performance improvements over the baseline BNL algorithm, there are research efforts toward achieving even better efficiency, in expectation. We note that still SFS may perform as many as $\mathcal{O}(n^2)$ dominance checks (as well as $\mathcal{O}(dn^2)$ primitive operations), depending on the dataset distribution. However, typically, the expected behavior results in a much smaller number of dominance checks.

First, we discuss the algorithm Linear Elimination Sort for Skyline (LESS) proposed in Godfrey et al. (2005). Initially, LESS performs a sorting of points in P using a topological order as SFS does. However, in addition to the main window used by SFS, LESS utilizes another window which is called the Elimination Filter (EF) and it is activated early to discard

---

Algorithm 2.3 Sort Filter Skyline (SFS)

Input : set of points P, monotone function $f()$
Output : the skyline of P ($SKY(P)$)

1: $SKY(P) = \emptyset$
2: sort P based on $f()$ /* *let p_i be the i-th point in the order* */
3: $i \leftarrow 1$
4: $SKY(P) \leftarrow SKY(P) \cup p_i$ /* *the first point in order is a skyline point* */
5: $i \leftarrow i + 1$
6: **while** $i \leq n$ **do**
7:   **if** $\nexists\ p \in SKY(P) : p \prec p_i$ **then**
8:     $SKY(P) \leftarrow SKY(P) \cup p_i$ /* *update skyline result* */
9:   **end if**
10:   $i \leftarrow i + 1$
11: **end while**
12: **return** $SKY(P)$

---

as many points as possible. The contents of EF are points from P with the best entropy score. It is expected that these points will dominate many points from P, reducing the cost of the subsequent steps.

EF is activated during the initial pass of the external sorting algorithm. Essentially, EF contains replicas of points with good entropy score. When the next block B of points is fetched from secondary memory, all points in B are checked against points in EF. In particular, if a point in B is dominated by any point in EF, then it is discarded. Next, from the points in B that have survived, the one with the best entropy score is selected (e.g., p_{best}). Any point in EF that is dominated by p_{best} is evicted from EF. Then, if EF is allowed to accommodate more points (based on the capacity of EF), p_{best} is added to EF. However, if EF is full, then p_{best} replaces the point in EF with the worst entropy score. If this is not possible, EF is not modified at all.

Another extension of SFS, proposed in Bartolini et al. (2006), is the SaLSa algorithm (Sort and Limit Skyline algorithm), where the number of required dominance checks is significantly reduced in comparison to the previous algorithms. SaLSa is based on the observation that if the set of points P is sorted based on a convenient order according to a monotone function, then $SKY(P)$ may be determined without the need to scan the whole set P. Therefore, in contrast to SFS and LESS, SaLSa supports *early termination*, resulting in less dominance checks in comparison to the previous alternatives. The main idea behind early termination is the following: let p_{best} be a convenient point that has been selected from P, and let P' be the subset of P that has not been checked by the algorithm based on the order posed by the monotone function $f()$. The algorithm may terminate if p_{best} is guaranteed to dominate all points in P'. This means that all points in P' are contained in the dominance region of p_{best}.

The performance of the SaLSa algorithm depends heavily on two important factors: (i) the monotone function used to sort points in P; and (ii) the way to determine how early termination will be achieved. As in the case of SFS and LESS, the worst-case complexity of SaLSa remains $\mathcal{O}(dn^2)$. However, the algorithm behaves much better in practice.

Divide and Conquer (DC)

A divide-and-conquer algorithm for skyline queries was proposed in Kung et al. (1975); Preparata and Shamos (1985). This algorithm computes the median value in a dimension, and divides the underlying space into two partitions P_1, P_2. Then, it computes the skyline results S_1, S_2 of P_1, P_2, respectively, by recursively dividing P_1 and P_2. The recursive partitioning terminates when there is only one (or a few) object(s) remaining. The overall skyline is computed by merging S_1 and S_2, and by eliminating the objects of S_2 which are dominated by any object of S_1. The worst-case complexity is: $O(n(\log n)^{(d-2)}) + O(n \log n)$, where d is the dimensionality. Variants of DC have been proposed in Börzsönyi et al. (2001) for the case that a partitioning does not fit into the main memory. These variants are based on an m-way partitioning, where instead of dividing the space into two partitions only, the idea is to divide it into m partitions in such a way that every partition can be accommodated in the available memory.

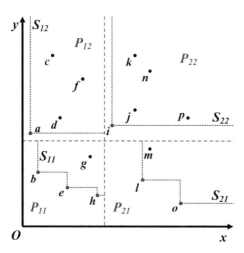

Figure 2.3: Divide and conquer algorithm example.

Figure 2.3 depicts a partitioning of the space into four partitions $P_{11}, P_{12}, P_{21}, P_{22}$. The partial skylines are $S_{11} = \{b, e, h\}, S_{12} = \{a\}, S_{21} = \{l, o\}, S_{22} = \{i\}$, respectively. To obtain the final skyline S, we need to remove the points that are dominated by some point in other partitions. It is evident that all points in the skyline of P_{11} must appear in the final skyline as well, whereas those in P_{22} are discarded immediately because they are dominated by all points in P_{11}. The skyline points in P_{12} are compared only with points in P_{11}, because no point in P_{22} or P_{21} can dominate those in P_{12}. In this example, point a is not dominated by b, e, h, thus it is included in the final skyline $SKY(P)$. Similarly, the skyline of P_{21} is also compared with points in P_{11}, which results in the removal of l. Finally, the algorithm terminates and returns the skyline set $SKY(P) = \{a, b, e, h, o\}$.

Another interesting variation of DC is an optimal algorithm named (DCSkyline) for computing the skyline in two-dimensional spaces, proposed in Lu et al. (2003).

Bitmap-based Skylines

An algorithm based in bitmap encodings has been proposed in Tan et al. (2001). Each object is mapped to an m-bit vector, where m is the sum of the total number of distinct values from each of d dimensions. More specifically, if k_i is the total number of distinct values on the ith dimension, then $m = \sum_{i=1}^{d} k_i$. Assume that there are k_i distinct values on the ith dimension and they are ordered ascending. Then, the j_ith smallest value is represented by k_i bits, where the leftmost $k_i - j_i + 1$ bits are 1 and the remaining bits are 0.

Let us compute the bitmap encodings for an example set P in the two-dimensional space. In the x dimension we have 14 distinct values: 1, 2, 4, 5, 6, 8, 9, 10, 12, 15, 16, 17, 21, 22, whereas

Table 2.1: Bitmap encodings example

Point	Bitmap Representation
$a(1, 12)$	(11111111111111, 11111110000000)
$b(2, 7)$	(11111111111110, 11111111110000)
$c(4, 22)$	(11111111111100, 10000000000000)
$d(5, 14)$	(11111111111000, 11111000000000)
$e(6, 5)$	(11111111110000, 11111111111100)
$f(8, 19)$	(11111111100000, 11100000000000)
$g(9, 9)$	(11111111000000, 11111111100000)
$h(10, 4)$	(11111110000000, 11111111111110)
$i(12, 13)$	(11111100000000, 11111100000000)
$j(15, 15)$	(11111000000000, 11110000000000)
$k(15, 22)$	(11111000000000, 10000000000000)
$l(16, 6)$	(11110000000000, 11111111111000)
$m(17, 10)$	(11100000000000, 11111111000000)
$n(17, 20)$	(11100000000000, 11000000000000)
$o(21, 3)$	(11000000000000, 11111111111111)
$p(22, 14)$	(10000000000000, 11111000000000)

in the y dimension we have also 14 distinct values: 3, 4, 5, 6, 7, 9, 10, 12, 13, 14, 15, 19, 20, 22. Therefore, each dimension is encoded with 14 bits (in total $m = 28$). Table 2.1 depicts the final encodings. To decide whether a point (x, y) belongs to the skyline, the algorithm creates two bit-strings s_x, s_y by juxtaposing the right-most corresponding bits (of the order of x and y in the corresponding dimensions), from the encodings of every point, and check if there is only one 1 in the result of the bit-string $s_x \& s_y$. For example, for point $h(10, 4)$ we must take the 8th right-most bit from the x-encodings and the 2nd right-most bit from the y-encodings. Thus, s_x = 1111111100000000 and s_y = 0000000100000010, which results in $s_x \& s_y$ = 0000000100000000 meaning that point h is included in the skyline. For the point $g(9, 9)$ we must take the 7th right-most bit from the x-encodings and the 6th right-most bit from the y-encodings. Therefore, s_x = 1111111000000000 and s_y = 0100101100010010; thus, $s_x \& s_y$ = 0100101000000000 which means that point g is not a member of $SKY(P)$. The same operations are repeated for every point in the dataset, to obtain the final skyline result.

2.2.2   INDEX-BASED TECHNIQUES

The common characteristic of the algorithms presented in the previous section is that they provide the skyline result without using an indexing mechanism. An index facilitates fast access to specific parts of the database without scanning irrelevant subsets of the data that cannot contribute to the final result. In general, the use of an index on specific attributes may improve the runtime performance of selection and join queries in database systems by orders of magnitude.

Skyline Computation with B-trees

The B-tree by Comer (1979) is one of the most fundamental secondary memory access method being used consistently in database management systems. A skyline processing algorithm based in B-trees for two-dimensional data has been proposed in Börzsönyi et al. (2001), where the data have two ordered indices, e.g., a B-tree or a B^+-tree, for each dimension of the underlying space. The algorithm computes a superset of the skyline by scanning simultaneously through both indices and terminates as soon as an object p has been found in both indices. This is the first step of Fagin's A_0 algorithm that has been proposed in Fagin (1996). Any object which has not been inspected in both indices is definitely not part of the skyline, because it is dominated by p. Therefore, candidate objects are those which have been already inspected in at least one index; these objects are kept in a separate set S (the superset of the skyline set $SKY(P)$). Finally, any of the previous algorithms can be executed in S to find the skyline. This algorithm can be generalized for more than two dimensions, as proposed in Tan et al. (2001). This algorithm is extended further in Balke et al. (2004); Lo et al. (2006) to support progressive query processing in distributed environments. In particular, the data are retrieved by sorted access only, and each data source (which can be in a different location in the web) is invoked in a round-robin fashion. In both studies (Balke et al., 2004; Lo et al., 2006), the same important property of this algorithm (used for pruning) has been presented and proved: after an object has been seen in each index (which is also referred as a *terminating object*) and all objects with equal values in each list have also been seen, then all remaining objects not yet seen cannot be part of the skyline, as they are dominated by the terminating object.

Figure 2.4 depicts a legal "screenshot" of the algorithm execution. The data are organized in two indices, one for dimension x and one for dimension y. Each index keeps the object identifier (id) and its corresponding value. The values are sorted in ascending order. During the round-robin scan the inspected objects are inserted into the set S. After nine value visits the object e has been detected in both x and y indices; thus, it is the terminating object. No more objects have equal values to 6 (which is the last accessed values on x and y). Therefore, $S = \{a, b, c, d, e, h, l, o\}$, and all other objects not yet seen (f, g, i, j, k, m, n, p) can be discarded (as they are dominated by e). Then, we check S for dominance relationships: a dominates c, d, and h dominates l; thus, c, d, l are removed from S, and the final skyline result is $SKY(P) = \{a, b, e, h, o\}$.

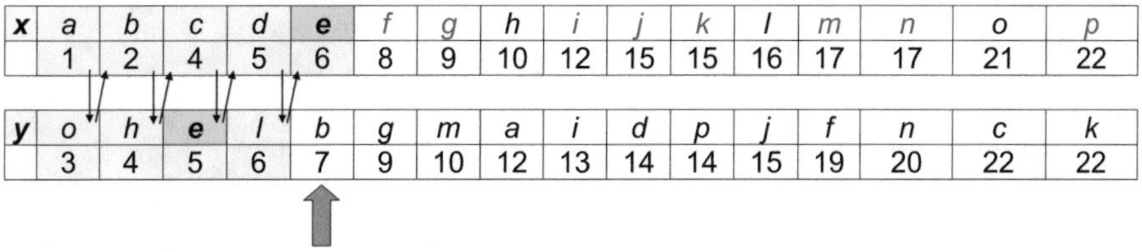

x	*a*	*b*	*c*	*d*	**e**	*f*	*g*	*h*	*i*	*j*	*k*	*l*	*m*	*n*	*o*	*p*
	1	2	4	5	6	8	9	10	12	15	15	16	17	17	21	22

y	*o*	*h*	**e**	*l*	*b*	*g*	*m*	*a*	*i*	*d*	*p*	*j*	*f*	*n*	*c*	*k*
	3	4	5	6	7	9	10	12	13	14	14	15	19	20	22	22

Figure 2.4: Progressive skyline example.

The major advantage of this algorithm is that it utilizes a widely used access method (the B-tree) and also it may invoke any algorithm to compute the skyline from the set S. On the other hand, the algorithm is sensitive to the number of dimensions. The number of indexing structures used equals the number of dimensions which can be significantly larger that 2 or 3.

Skyline Computation with R-trees
A spatial index, e.g., an R-tree, can be used to compute the skyline, as proposed in Börzsönyi et al. (2001). The R-tree involves all dimensions of the objects, thus it can be used only when all dimensions are considered into the skyline query. The R-tree is traversed in a DFS way, whereas branches and regions dominated by any candidate object are pruned. However, in Börzsönyi et al. (2001) the idea of using a spatial index for skyline computation was presented as future work. Later, other researchers investigated this topic and reported algorithms for skyline computation based on spatial access methods.

Before presenting some fundamental algorithms for skyline computation using an R-tree, a brief introduction to R-trees follows, to keep the chapter (and the book) self-contained. The R-tree was proposed by Antonin Guttman in Guttman (1984) to organize efficiently large sets of small rectangles in VLSI chip design. An R-tree can organize a set of d-dimensional objects (usually rectangles or points). It may also organize more complex geometric objects like polygons. However, since a polygon may contain an arbitrary number of points, usually each polygon is represented by its Minimum Bounding Rectangle (MBR).

An R-tree is a secondary memory access method which is composed of a root node, internal nodes and leaves. All leaf nodes appear at the same level and each node has the same capacity (e.g., 32 KB). Each node of the R-tree corresponds to the MBR that bounds its children. The tree leaves contain pointers to the database records (or objects) instead of pointers to children nodes. An R-tree of order (m, M) has the following properties.

- Each leaf node (if it is not the root) can accommodate at most M entries, whereas the minimum allowed number of entries is $m \leq M/2$. Each entry is of the form (mbr, oid), such that mbr is the MBR that spatially contains the object and oid is the object's identifier.

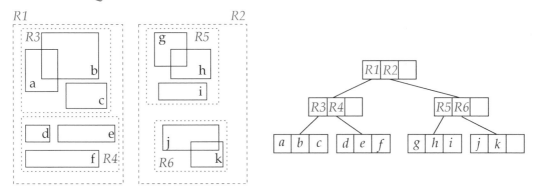

Figure 2.5: A set of rectangles (left) and an R-tree (right).

- The number of entries that each internal node can accommodate is again between $m \leq M/2$ and M. Each node contains entries of the form (mbr, ptr), where ptr is a "pointer" to a child node and mbr is the MBR that spatially contains the MBRs of the corresponding child.

- The minimum allowed number of entries in the root node is 2, unless it is a leaf or an internal node.

- All leaves of the R-tree lie at the same tree level.

An example R-tree is shown in Figure 2.5 which organizes a set of rectangles in the 2-dimensional space. It is evident that the R-tree performs a hierarchical decomposition where the level of detail increases as we move from the root to the leaf level. For example, the root node contains the entries R_1 and R_2 which provide a very vague representation of the underlying objects. On the other hand, R_3, R_4, R_5, and R_6 offer a more detailed representation. Finally, the nodes located at the leaf level contain the data elements (rectangles in this example).

The R-tree is a *dynamic* access method as it supports insertions, deletions, and updates. With respect to search operations, it supports range search, nearest-neighbor search as well as joins. The R-tree has been used extensively toward the design of more complex algorithms on top of multi-dimensional objects, usually points and rectangles as mentioned in Manolopoulos et al. (2006). Because of its good expected behavior, it has also been used to speed-up skyline query processing. In the sequel we present two algorithmic techniques that exploit R-trees for more efficient computation.

(A) Nearest Neighbor Skyline Algorithm (NNS)
The first complete skyline algorithm based on a spatial index, e.g., an R-tree, is the NNS algorithm, proposed in Kossmann et al. (2002). It is called NNS due to its relevance to nearest neighbor search. It identifies skyline objects by a repeated NN search using a suitable distance

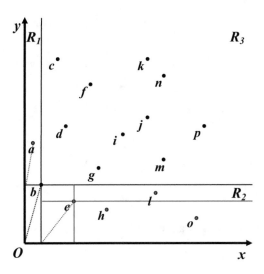

Figure 2.6: NNS algorithm example.

measure. The algorithm iteratively determines the nearest-neighbor point from the origin in a given region of space, based on any monotone distance function, e.g., the Euclidean distance.

During the algorithm execution, entire regions dominated by a candidate object are discarded, and regions that cannot be discarded are added to a *to-do list* for further space partitioning. For example, when the NN object to the origin is detected (object b in Figure 2.6), region R_3 can be discarded because all contained objects are dominated by b, and regions R_1 and R_2 are added to the list for further partitioning. Continuing our example, the NN object to the origin of R_1 is a and is the only object, thus there are no other objects to discard or perform any further partitioning. The NN object to the origin of R_2 is e, and by further partitioning we can discard object l. The region of objects h, o is remaining in the list and by further partitioning the objects cannot be discarded. The list becomes empty and, thus, the algorithm terminates. The final skyline contains all objects that have not been discarded, i.e., $SKY(P) = \{a, b, e, h, o\}$.

The NNS algorithm was further optimized in Kossmann et al. (2002) for online environments, where the first skyline objects are reported immediately to the user, and the algorithm produces additional results continuously, allowing the user to give preferences during the running time to control the output priority of the next results.

(B) Branch and Bound Skyline Algorithm (BBS)
Like NNS, the Branch and Bound Skyline (BBS) algorithm proposed in Papadias et al. (2003) is also based on nearest neighbor search. It is a progressive (it reports the skyline objects progressively) and I/O efficient algorithm. An R-tree is used for indexing, and the main distance

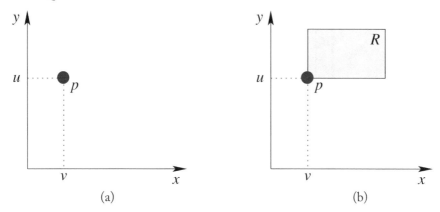

Figure 2.7: Distance from a point and a rectangle to the origin.

measure used is the L_1 distance. A minheap structure Q (a priority queue) is used for the processing, which keeps intermediate node entries or data entries with their corresponding *minimum distance from the origin*, and a set $SKY(P)$ for the skyline objects. The minimum distance of a node with an MBR is the sum of the coordinates of its lower-left corner (i.e., the L_1 distance from the origin). This concept is shown in Figure 2.7. In both cases, the distance from the point p or the rectangle R to the origin equals $v + u$, which is the L_1 distance of p to the origin.

Initially, Q contains all entries of the root of the R-tree, and $SKY(P)$ is empty. While the heap is not empty, the top entry e of Q is removed, and if e is dominated by some object in $SKY(P)$ then e is discarded. Otherwise, in case that e is an intermediate node, each child e_i of e is checked if it is dominated or not by some point in $SKY(P)$, and if not then e_i is inserted in Q. In case that e is a data node, then any contained object which is not dominated by some point in $SKY(P)$ is also inserted in $SKY(P)$. The algorithm terminates when the heap is empty and, thus, the final skyline result $SKY(P)$ is returned.

One of the most important properties of the BBS algorithm is that when the top of the heap contains a data point, then this point is guaranteed to be a skyline point if it is not dominated by some point in $SKY(P)$. Next we present an example of the BBS execution.

Assume that the points of P are organized in a simple R-tree with a node capacity of four (4) entries as depicted in Figure 2.8. The R-tree has only two levels, the root node R and the data nodes N_1, N_2, N_3, N_4. The BBS algorithm starts from the root node R and inserts all of its entries into the heap Q with their corresponding minimum distances, i.e., $Q = \{(N_1,6),(N_2,13),(N_3,19),(N_4,25)\}$. Initially, $SKY(P) = \emptyset$. Node N_1 is the top heap object, thus it is expanded and all of its points are inserted into the heap with their minimum distances (N_1 is removed), i.e., $Q = \{(b,9),(e,11),(N_2,13),(h,14),(g,18), (N_3,19),(N_4,25)\}$.

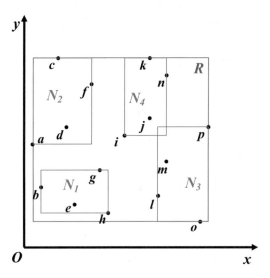

Figure 2.8: BBS algorithm example.

Point b is the top heap object and, thus, it is removed from Q and is inserted directly in $SKY(P)$ (i.e., $SKY(P) = \{b\}$). Next, e is removed from Q and since it is not dominated by b, it is inserted into $SKY(P)$.

Thus, at this point we have $SKY(P) = \{b, e\}$. The current state of Q is: $Q = \{(N_2,13),(h,14),(g,18),(N_3,19),(N_4,25)\}$. Next, node N_2 is the top heap object; thus, it is expanded and all of its points are checked for dominance against the points of $SKY(P)$. Therefore, a is inserted into Q, whereas c, d and g are discarded because they are dominated by b. The contents of Q at this point are: $Q = \{(a,13),(h,14),(g,18),(N_3,19),(N_4,25)\}$.

Now point a is the top heap object, thus, it is removed from Q and inserted into $SKY(P)$ ($SKY(P) = \{b, e, a\}$) since it is not dominated by $SKY(P)$. Then, point h is the top heap object, thus, it is removed from Q and it is inserted in $SKY(P)$ ($SKY(P) = \{a, b, e, h\}$) because it is not dominated. The next element to be extracted from Q is g, which is dominated by b and c and thus, it is rejected. At this point $Q = \{(N_3,19),(N_4,25)\}$. The algorithm next will process N_3, inserting o into $SKY(P)$, whereas N_4 is rejected since it is dominated by at least one skyline point. Since the heap Q is empty, the algorithm terminates and the final skyline result is $SKY(P) = \{a, b, e, h, o\}$).

One very important feature of BBS is that it is I/O optimal. More specifically, given an R-tree, BBS will access as few nodes of the R-tree as possible. This characteristic is significant because it guarantees that the algorithm will perform the minimum number of disk accesses to compute the skyline result, than any other algorithm that uses the same R-tree. Performance

---

Algorithm 2.4 Branch-and-Bound Skyline (BBS)

Input : set of points P, an R-tree index *Rtree*
Output : the skyline of P $(SKY(P))$

1: $SKY(P) \leftarrow \emptyset$
2: initialize priority queue Q
3: $root \leftarrow$ the root node of *Rtree*
4: insert all entries of $root$ in Q
5: **while** Q is not empty **do**
6:      $e \leftarrow Q.removeTop()$ */* get the closest entry to the origin */
7:      **if** e is dominated by a point in $SKY(P)$ **then**
8:          discard e
9:      **else**
10:         **if** e belongs to an intermediate node **then**
11:             **for all** e_i where e_i is in the child node of e **do**
12:                 **if** e_i is not dominated by any point of $SKY(P)$ **then**
13:                     $Q.insert(e_i)$
14:                 **end if**
15:             **end for**
16:         **else**
17:             */* e is a data element, update the skyline result */
18:             **if** e is not dominated by $SKY(P)$ **then**
19:                 $SKY(P) \leftarrow SKY(P) \cup \{e\}$
20:             **end if**
21:         **end if**
22:     **end if**
23: **end while**
24: **return** $SKY(P)$

---

evaluation results reported in Papadias et al. (2003) have shown that BBS is in practice significantly more efficient than NNS by several orders of magnitude.

BBS is based on an important property of the skyline. The best point p based on any
monotone function on the attribute values is guaranteed to be contained in the skyline result. It
is evident that the first point that enters the skyline result is the point with the minimum distance
from the origin. Based on the previous observation, this is true for any monotone function.

In Luo et al. (2004), an R-tree-based algorithm is proposed, which is a variation of BBS
that adopts a DFS technique with a *forward checking* based on a *region-dominance* relation to

reduce space complexity. The algorithm is I/O optimal and requires logarithmic space in the worst case in the two-dimensional space, if there are not many overlapping rectangles in the R-tree structure.

2.3   ADVANCED SKYLINE PROCESSING

In addition to the aforementioned main-memory and secondary-memory skyline processing techniques, the related literature is rich in parallel/distributed approaches as well as skyline algorithms in dynamic environments. The exploitation of multiple resources as well as the careful handling of insertions/deletions plays a very important role toward scalable skyline computation.

2.3.1   DISTRIBUTED AND PARALLEL TECHNIQUES

The use of multiple resources is one alternative to guarantee scalable query processing. As in other types of queries, skyline queries may benefit significantly from parallel or distributed approaches. The algorithmic techniques studied in Balke et al. (2004); Lo et al. (2006), which have already been presented previously as index-based algorithms, can efficiently perform skyline queries in distributed environments. Another study that addresses the problem of parallelizing skyline query execution over a large number of machines by leveraging content-based data partitioning, is presented in Wu et al. (2006). The proposed distributed skyline query processing algorithm, named DSL, discovers the skyline points in a progressive manner.

Skyline query processing on Peer-to-Peer (P2P) networks is studied in Wang et al. (2007). A method named SSP is proposed which partitions and numbers the data space among the peer nodes such that the target subspace (region) number can be derived with good accuracy to control the peers accessed and search messages during skyline query processing. A generalization of the SSP method is the SKYFRAME method presented in Wang et al. (2009), which performs skyline processing without the need to determine the starting peer.

A study focused on the efficient processing of skyline queries in large-scale P2P systems, where it is nearly impossible to guarantee complete and exact query answers without exhaustive search, is presented in Hose (2005). Approximate algorithms with probabilistic guarantees are proposed to reduce the number of queried peers. Another similar approach was proposed in Li et al. (2006b), where approximate algorithms are proposed to support skyline queries where exact answers are too costly to obtain. The proposed algorithms produce high quality results by using heuristics based on local semantics of peer nodes. Moreover, a detailed survey for skyline processing in highly distributed environments is presented in Hose and Vlachou (2011).

In Vlachou et al. (2007, 2010), a threshold-based algorithm for efficient subspace skyline processing in a P2P environment is proposed, called SKYPEER, which forwards the skyline query requests among peers, in such a way that the amount of data transferred over the network connecting the peers is significantly reduced.

Skyline query processing techniques in Mobile Ad-Hoc Networks (MANETs) are studied in Huang et al. (2006a), where the main focus is to reduce the communication cost among mobile devices and reduce the execution time on each single mobile device. Query processing and optimization techniques in wireless sensor networks are also studied in Li and Xiong (2010). In the later work, the SKY-SEARCH algorithm was proposed, which computes the skyline with the highest existential probability in a computational and energy-efficient way.

In the sequel, we study in detail a parallel skyline query processing technique proposed in Vlachou et al. (2008) that has been designed to work in shared-nothing architectures. The abstract architecture comprises a master node that takes the role of the *coordinator* and a set of *worker* nodes. The role of the coordinator is to accept queries and delegate jobs to the associated workers. For the rest of the discussion the number of servers will be denoted by N. It is assumed that all machines communicate through a high-speed network. This means that network latency must be taken into account.

The set of d-dimensional points P comprising the dataset of interest has to be partitioned across the N servers. Each partition P_i contains a subset of the points of P, where $1 \leq i \leq N$. A convenient data partitioning scheme is essential toward efficient parallel processing. The algorithm is composed of three phases.

- *Partitioning Phase*: the data elements are distributed across the available worker nodes.

- *Local Processing Phase*: each worker computes the skyline based in its local data only.

- *Merging Phase*: the coordinator computes the final skyline result based on local results produced by the workers in the previous phase.

Once the partitioning strategy has been decided, the rest of the processing (local processing and merging) is straightforward. Therefore, let us focus on different partitioning alternatives aiming at determining the impact on the overall query processing. The most trivial partitioning strategy, which is also the most flexible, is the *Random Partitioning* (RP), where each worker receives almost the same amount of points whereas points are distributed randomly (or using a hash function, or using round-robin). Another partitioning strategy that is very easy to apply is the *Grid-based Partitioning* (GP), where the address space is divided to cells and each worker receives the points falling on a specific cell. However, we may allow that a worker may receive more than one cells to handle. The partitioning strategy proposed in Vlachou et al. (2008) is the *Angle-based Partitioning* (AP) which divides the address space into conical regions with respect to the origin of the coordinate system.

Before we analyze the impact of each partitioning strategy, we give an example demonstrating the difference between GP and AP in Figure 2.9. For simplicity, we assume that the grid decomposition must guarantee that each cell must contain approximately the same number of points. Although this is not mandatory for the correctness of the algorithm, load imbalance may cause significant performance degradation. There are many grid structures that can be applied that are not necessarily uniform with respect to the size of each cell. Figure 2.9a depicts one way of decomposing the address space by applying a uniform grid partitioning, where each cell

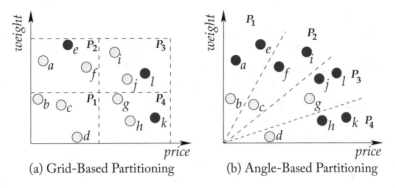

Figure 2.9: Examples of grid-based and angle-based partitioning.

contains three points. On the other hand, by applying an angle-based partitioning, the address space is decomposed, as shown in Figure 2.9b.

Assume further that there are four workers in the system, meaning that each worker is assigned one partition P_1, P_2, P_3, P_4. In the case of grid-based partitioning, each worker is assigned a cell and computes the *local skyline*. Similarly, when angle-based partitioning is used, each worker is assigned a separate conical region, and the same process is applied. Local skyline points are shown yellow in Figure 2.9.

The first observation is that the grid-based partitioning, shown in Figure 2.9a, produces more local sklyline results in total than that of the angle-based partitioning. Let S_i denote the local skyline set for partition P_i. As observed, the local skyline points returned by each worker are: $S_1 = \{b, c, d\}$, $S_2 = \{a, f\}$, $S_3 = \{i, j\}$ and $S_4 = \{g, h\}$. In other words, 9 out of 12 points of the input dataset are returned to the coordinator for producing the final result. The limitation of this effect is twofold: (i) more data will travel through the network increasing network latency and (ii) more work is required by the coordinator toward merging the local skyline points from each partition to produce the final skyline result. Moreover, in GP some workers may do unnecessary work. For example, the cell containing points i, j, and l should be eliminated in the first place since all points in this cell are dominated and therefore no point from this cell will appear in the final skyline result. On the other hand, in Figure 2.9b we observe that the local skyline points is significantly smaller by applying the angle-based partitioning strategy. More specifically, the local skyline results are: $S_1 = \{b\}$, $S_2 = \{c\}$, $S_3 = \{g\}$, and $S_4 = \{d\}$. In this case less network latency is expected and also less work is required by the coordinator for merging partial results.

Taking into account how grid-based and angle-based partitioning strategies are working, the RP strategy is expected to have the worst performance, since it does not follow any principled way of partitioning the data across workers. It is expected that RP will have a high network latency cost which has a direct negative impact on performance, and in fact this is verified by the experimental results reported in Vlachou et al. (2008). It is also verified that AP has the best performance among all partitioning strategies. In Vlachou et al. (2008), the authors also discuss about *equi-volume* angle-based partitioning (similar to a uniform grid) and *dynamic* angle-based partitioning (similar to an adaptive grid). In general, AP shows the best results with respect to runtime performance and also it shows great scalability by increasing the cardinality of the dataset and the dimensionality of the data.

2.3.2   SKYLINES IN DYNAMIC ENVIRONMENTS

In real-world applications, *dynamic* environments are the rule rather than the exception. In the majority of practical applications, datasets are dynamic in nature, which means that insertions and deletions of objects may take place, in general, arbitrarily. In particular, the following primitive operations need to be supported in a dynamic environment.

- The insertion of a new point p_{new} may result in changing the skyline set, since p_{new} may dominate some points in $SKY(P)$. In this case, p_{new} must be inserted into $SKY(P)$ and all points from $SKY(P)$ dominated by p_{new} must be removed.

- The deletion of an existing point p_{old} may result in changing the skyline set, since if p_{old} is part of $SKY(P)$, its deletion may promote dominated points into $SKY(P)$, if they are not dominated by any other point.

Evidently, depending on the coordinates of the inserted/deleted point, $SKY(P)$ may not be affected at all. However, if $SKY(P)$ needs to be updated, then these changes must be as efficient as possible. It is not hard to deduce that we can always apply one of the skyline algorithms presented previously after every insertion or deletion. For example, if BBS is being used for skyline computation, after the insertion of a new point (or the deletion of an existing one) BBS may run again to provide a fresh skyline result. However, such an approach is very computationally intensive and more incremental techniques are required.

Let us describe how the BBS algorithm (Papadias et al., 2005a) can be enhanced with an efficient update process to handle insertions and deletions. Recall that BBS works by using an R-tree index over the data points. Therefore, this index may be also utilized during updates. Let p_{new} be an incoming point. We identify the following cases.

- The new point p_{new} is dominated by at least one point of $SKY(P)$. In this case, p_{new} cannot affect the contents of $SKY(P)$.

- The new point p_{new} is not dominated by any point in $SKY(P)$ and it does not dominate any point in $SKY(P)$. In this case, p_{new} is simply inserted into $SKY(P)$.

- Finally, the new point p_{new} may dominate some points in $SKY(P)$. Let $W = \{p \in SKY(P) : p_{new} \prec p\}$, i.e., W contains all points in $SKY(P)$ dominated by p_{new}. In this case, $SKY(P)$ is updated by removing all points that belong to W and by inserting p_{new} in $SKY(P)$. An example of this case is depicted in Figure 2.10a.

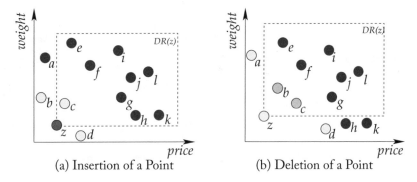

(a) Insertion of a Point   (b) Deletion of a Point

Figure 2.10: Examples of handling insertions and deletions.

Next, we focus on deletions. Let p_{old} be an existing point that is being deleted from the dataset P. The deletion is handled as follows.

- The point p_{old} is dominated by at least one skyline point of $SKY(P)$. In this case, no further actions are needed and $SKY(P)$ remains unchanged.

- The point p_{old} is part of $SKY(P)$, and evidently in this case it should be deleted from $SKY(P)$. In addition, if there are any points in P that are dominated by p_{old}, then some of these points must be inserted in $SKY(P)$. An example of this case is depicted in Figure 2.10b.

Let us describe briefly the two cases shown in Figure 2.10. Assume that point z is a new point and it is being inserted, as shown in Figure 2.10a. Currently, the skyline set is $SKY(P) = \{b, c, d\}$. The insertion of z forces the removal of c from the skyline, because $z \prec c$ (note that c lies inside the dominance region of z). In fact, we are not interested in other points dominated by z if they do not belong to the skyline. The final skyline result is $SKY(P) = \{b, z, d\}$. A deletion example is shown in Figure 2.10b, where initially $SKY(P) = \{a, z, d\}$ and the point z is being deleted. Again, we observe that the points b and c must be inserted into $SKY(P)$, since after the removal of z these points are not dominated by any other point in $SKY(P)$. Therefore, the final skyline set is $SKY(P) = \{a, b, c, d\}$.

In addition to the dynamic environments that handle insertions and deletions in an ad-hoc manner, several applications rely on *stream-based* processing, where the input data are highly dynamic and may arrive in arbitrary rates. In addition, processing is performed strictly in main memory due to the online nature of these applications and the high demands they pose with respect to efficiency. One of the streaming models suggests that there is a window containing the *active points*. This window may be defined based on the number of points we are interested or the time that the points were inserted, i.e., we can have a *count-based* or a *time-based* sliding window, respectively. In both cases, we need to support insertion of new points and expiration of existing (old) points.

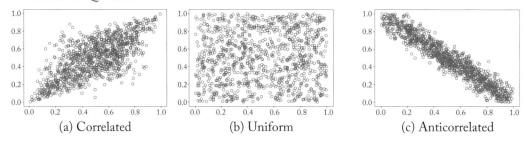

(a) Correlated   (b) Uniform   (c) Anticorrelated

Figure 2.11: Different data distributions (examples for the two-dimensional case).

In its simplest form, the number of active points is represented as a set P, where in every time instance a new point p_{new} arrives and an existing point $p_{old} \in P$ expires. Evidently, a more general case involves the insertion of more points, e.g., k and the expiration of k points. We assume a count-based window, where the cardinality of P remains constant.

A window-based algorithm for skyline queries is proposed in Yu et al. (2005), which transforms skyline queries into many different dynamic window queries. Another sliding window approach is proposed in Lin et al. (2005), which applies an effective pruning technique to minimize the number of elements to be kept. Sliding Window Skylines on Data Streams are studied also in Tao and Papadias (2006), where the proposed algorithms continuously monitor the incoming data and maintain the skyline incrementally.

A continuous skyline query involves not only static dimensions but also the dynamic ones. In such cases, a useful computation over streaming data sets is to produce a continuous and valid skyline summary over time. An efficient continuous time-interval skyline algorithm is proposed in Morse et al. (2007a). Another proposal for skyline queries for moving objects is presented in Huang et al. (2006b), where a kinetic-based data structure is applied to facilitate query processing.

2.4   SKYLINE CARDINALITY

The skyline query does not require any input from the user, except for the preferences for minimizing or maximizing attribute values. However, this simplicity of the query formulation comes with some significant consequences. The first important observation is that there is absolutely no guarantee about the cardinality of the skyline set $SKY(P)$. More formally, it holds that $1 \leq |SKY(P)| \leq |P|$.

The question is which factors affect the cardinality of $SKY(P)$. First, we will focus on the data distribution. Figure 2.11 presents three different data distributions in the two-dimensional space (correlated, uniform, anticorrelated). Evidently, these are not the only data distributions that may characterize the underlying dataset, but they are the most widely used to evaluate the performance of skyline query processing algorithms. The correlated distribution, shown in

Figure 2.11a, is the most *easy* to handle, because the cardinality of the skyline result is relatively small. In this distribution, high x values imply high y values and vice versa. This situation is very convenient, since in the extreme case all points will fit a straight line crossing the origin, which means that essentially the problem becomes one-dimensional. However, this *extreme* correlated distribution is very unlikely to appear in a real-world application.

A data distribution that often is being used as the *baseline* distribution is the uniform, shown in Figure 2.11b. It is expected that in this case the cardinality of $SKY(P)$ will be higher than that of the correlated distribution. Although the uniform distribution is not met in practice, it is often used because it leads to simplifications in analysis.

The most challenging data distribution, however, is the anticorrelated distribution which is shown in Figure 2.11c. One may observe that the *front* in this distribution is wider, which essentially means that the cardinality of the skyline set may be significantly larger than the previous cases. The main characteristic of the anticorrelated distribution which affects the performance of all skyline processing algorithms is the fact that high values in one dimension provide low values in the other. In its extreme case, all data points may fit on an almost straight line, which means that $SKY(P) = P$, i.e., all points are skyline points. Again, as in the case of the extreme correlated case, the extreme anticorrelated case is not realistic. However, still the anticorrelated distribution may return a large number of points, which may correspond to a significant proportion of P.

Another factor that affects the cardinality of the skyline result is the number of dimensions (d). The dimensionality of the dataset depends on the application and the origin of the raw data. Assume that we fix the data distribution, and compute the skyline for two point sets in d and $d + 1$ dimensions, respectively. Then we expect that $|SKY(P_d)| \leq |SKY(P_{d+1})|$. For example, earlier in this chapter we have discussed about skylines when $d = 1$ and $d = 2$ and we noted that in one-dimensional data (assuming that all values are unique) there is only one skyline point and this does not depend at all on the data distribution. However, for $d = 2$ the number of skyline points increases. In addition to this observation we can provide a more formal investigation regarding the number of the skyline points for different values of d. Let n be the number of points in P and d be the number of dimensions. Assume further, without loss of generality, that the coordinates of the points in each dimensions are integers in the range $[1, n]$. By assuming that all $(n!)^d$ relative orderings are equally probable, for a fixed d, the average number of points in the skyline result is $\mathcal{O}((\ln n)^{d-1})$. This result has been reported in Bentley et al. (1978), and provides an estimate of the cardinality of $SKY(P)$ under certain assumptions. A tighter upper bound was reported in Buchta (1989), where the authors proved that the skyline cardinality is in $\Theta((\ln n)^{d-1}/(d - 1)!)$. Other research efforts to provide more accurate estimations include the works of Godfrey (2004) and Tiakas et al. (2013). An accurate estimation of the number of skyline points is very important in cost estimation and therefore in the query optimization process in general.

Definitely, in some cases the cardinality of the skyline result will be significantly large. For example, as reported in Börzsönyi et al. (2001), for a set of 100,000 points in the ten-dimensional space, if the points follow a uniform distribution, then the number of skyline points is around 25,000, whereas if the points obey an anticorrelated distribution then the number of skyline points is around 75,000. It is evident that in both cases the number of returned results is significantly high to be inspected manually. Therefore, a natural question arises: is there a way to reduce the number of returned skyline results? In fact, there are several different directions one may follow toward reducing the number of returned results. Some of these directions are described briefly below.

- The number of skyline points returned may be reduced by incorporating an additional ranking criterion over the set $SKY(P)$ as mentioned in Valkanas et al. (2014). For example, a ranking function may be applied on all points in $SKY(P)$ and the best k points may be returned. For example, this ranking function may compute the number of points dominated by each skyline point.

- A second approach that one can follow is to compute the skyline in a subset of the dimensions as suggested in Tao et al. (2006); Xia et al. (2012). In high dimensional spaces, it is expected that the probability that a point p dominates another point q (under uniformity and independence assumptions) is reduced. Therefore, selecting a subset of $d' < d$ dimensions will effectively lead to a reduction in the number of skyline points returned.

- Another alternative is to select the most representative skyline points, based on *diversity* criteria as suggested in Tao (2009); Valkanas et al. (2013). This approach returns skyline points that have a high degree of diversity (i.e., non-similarity). For example, two skyline points that are very close to each other may not provide significant knowledge than two skyline points that are far apart.

In general, the skyline query is very useful with many practical applications, requiring only limited input from the user. However, there are many variations that have been proposed in the literature. Many of these variations are discussed in the following chapter.

2.5   SUMMARY

The skyline query is the simplest and the most widely used among all dominance-based queries. In this chapter, we presented the most important concepts and algorithmic techniques related to skyline query processing, by using different viewpoints. Given a set P of multi-dimensional points, the skyline query returns the set $SKY(P) \subseteq P$ containing points that are not dominated.

In case the whole data collection fits in main memory, evidently, query processing may be performed more efficiently. However, the rule is that the dataset is significantly larger than the amount of the available main memory. Therefore, efficient techniques are required to compute the skyline for disk-resident data. An orthogonal dimension is whether an index is available or not. In many cases, an index exists to support other queries, such range queries or nearest-neighbor queries. In such a case the index may be also used to accelerate the processing of skyline queries (e.g., the BBS algorithm). If no index is available, then different algorithmic techniques should be applied (e.g., SFS).

To be able to allow skyline computation in big datasets, parallel, distributed, and dynamic algorithms may be applied. These techniques provide the necessary speed-up in cases where single-processor algorithms are not able to guarantee efficient processing.

Although skyline processing has many advantages, there is one disadvantage that requires special attention: the number of skyline points cannot be controlled. In fact, the number of skyline points depends on the number of dimensions and the data distribution. To control the number of results several alternatives have been proposed. Some of them simply impose another criterion on top of the skyline result, whereas some others change the definition of dominance or apply different techniques to reduce the number of results if necessary. Some of these techniques are investigated in subsequent chapters.

CHAPTER 3

Variations of Skyline Queries

Skyline queries have earned a lot of attention due to their very wide application base in various domains such as multi-preference analysis and decision making. To better cater to application requirements, a number of research teams have put forward proposals for an extension of the definition of skyline on the basis of variants of the dominance relationship. In view of the increase in the number of variants put forward, this chapter examines how the conventional skyline query has been extended to produce different variants of dominant-based queries. It looks at the several properties that are preserved in a variant of the dominance relationship so that, while the original advantages are maintained, the flexibility to adapt to new applications is extended. It also looks at new dominance relationships that have been put forward and that were obtained by modifying some of the properties of the traditional dominance relationship.

The chapter begins by discussing the families of the k-dominant and skycube queries, which operate mainly on the basis of static data attributes (i.e., on objects, the attribute vectors of which are fixed), and subsequently goes on to discussing the family of the dynamic skyline queries, as well as the families of the spatial, metric and range-based skyline queries, which operate on dynamic attributes of the data. Last, for the sake of reference, a wide set of other types of variants of skyline and dominance-based queries is also briefly mentioned.

3.1 K-DOMINANT SKYLINE QUERIES

An advantage of the traditional skyline query is that it can be put to use in many decision-making applications. However, as the number of dimensions increases, the number of skyline points becomes too large for the issuer of the query to gain a helpful insight in response to the query. The reason for this is that the increase in the number of dimensions means that the chances of one point dominating another point decrease. The *k-dominant skyline query* deals with this problem in an effective way whereby, instead of being better in all the d dimensions, a point only needs to be better in some $k < d$ dimensions to dominate another point. Therefore, a point p is said to k-dominate another point r if there are k dimensions in which p is better than or equal to r and is better in at least one of these k dimensions. Thus, the k-dominant skyline query can find important and meaningful skyline points in high dimensional spaces by adjusting the well-established idea of dominance to k-dominance. Hence, a point that is not k-dominated by any other point is said to belong to the k-dominant skyline. The k attributes are not fixed and can be any subset of the d skyline attributes.

Table 3.1: Movie rating dataset

Movie ID	$Expert_1$	$Expert_2$	$Expert_3$	$Expert_4$
m_1	5	5	3	4
m_2	2	1	3	3
m_3	4	2	4	4
m_4	3	5	1	4
m_5	4	1	5	4

An example might be a person looking for top-rated movies on the basis of ratings given by experts, as shown in Table 3.1. In this case, the rating of every one of the experts, expert1, expert2, expert3, and expert4 corresponds to one dimension of the dataset. In more general terms, given a large number of experts, the dataset will consequently be a high-dimensional dataset. The skyline of the dataset in the above example is the set $\{m1, m3, m5\}$ and it contains top-rated movies, while movies that are consistently ranked below other movies, such as movie $m2$, are pruned away. This means that a movie is only considered to be better than another movie if it is given by all the experts a rating value higher than or the same as that other movie. While this is quite possible in the case of a small number of experts, it is much less likely in the case of a larger number of experts, since it only takes one outlier opinion to invalidate the dominance relationship. In the example given in Table 3.1, it is clear that the skyline set covers a large part of the whole dataset. As a result, the traditional skyline query is not able to recommend the most popular movies for users.

Alternatively, on the basis of the k-dominance relationship definition, movie m_1 is said to 4-dominate movie m_2 across the entire space $\{expert_1, expert_2, expert_3, expert_4\}$ and it 3-dominates m_3 across the subspace $\{expert_1, expert_2, expert_4\}$. The 4-dominant skyline set is actually the conventional skyline set, i.e., the set $\{m_1, m_3, m_5\}$, since none of these three movies is 4-dominated by any other movie in the dataset. Therefore, in the general setting the conventional skyline represents a special case of the k-dominant skyline, where $k = d$.

To achieve a tighter set of results, it is reasonable to consider that a movie will be rated higher than another if a number of $k < 4$ experts rate it higher. Therefore, the 3-dominant skyline query is a desired criterion, in which only movie m_1 is retrieved. Thus, the 3-dominant skyline query could identify the movie that best matches the search by adopting the parameter k. Moreover, Chan et al. (2006) proved that the k-dominant skyline is a subset of the original skyline. However, the chance of a point being excluded from a k-dominant skyline is more likely than it being excluded from the conventional skyline, since more points will be k-dominated than d-dominated. It has also been proved that the smaller the k, the smaller the resulting size of the k-dominant skyline query set will be. For example, it is worth noting that all the movies in Table 3.1 are 2-dominated by at least one other movie, consequently the query result for the

2-dominant skyline query is empty. Therefore, it is reasonable to say that the k-dominant skyline query has a large application base.

In Chan et al. (2006), the authors propose three algorithms to address the k-dominant skyline computation problem. The first is a one-scan algorithm, which computes the k-dominant skyline set by actually computing the traditional skyline set on the basis of all the d dimensions of the space and uses it to prune away non-k-dominated skyline points. As the entire set of points that belong to the traditional skyline can be large, keeping them all in main memory can be avoided by means of a two-scan algorithm. In the first scan, a candidate set of k-dominant skyline points is computed progressively by comparing every data point with the computed points in this candidate points set. The second scan verifies whether these points are truly k dominant skyline points. This method turns out to be much more efficient than the one-scan method. Finally, the paper proposes an algorithm called *sorted retrieval algorithm*, which pre-sorts the data points separately according to every dimension and then "merges" these ranked lists.

The approach of Zhang et al. (2009a) solves the same problem by organizing the current k-dominant skyline points in a search tree which defines a recursive space partitioning. With the help of this tree, every candidate k-dominant skyline point only needs to be compared with a small subset of the existing k-dominant skyline points. Lee et al. (2010) also contributed to the computation of this problem by organizing the dataset and the k-dominant skyline candidates using an index structure which exploits the clustering property of the Z-order curve. The framework they propose consists of a two-face approach that initially filters the dataset to select the k-dominant candidate points, which are then re-examined to remove false hits.

To deal with datasets that are continuously updated while multiple k-dominant skyline queries are executed concurrently, Kontaki et al. (2008) propose a method which divides the space in pairs of dimensions. For every pair, a grid is constructed to compute the skyline points for these dimensions. Then, the method exploits the discovered skyline points to eliminate candidate k-dominant skyline points and combines the partial results to obtain the final result. The method can handle multiple continuous queries, every one of which may be defined in a subset of the available dimensions, since different users might express an interest in different attributes. Moreover, the parameter k set by every query can take a different value.

The case of incomplete data is also an interesting application. For example, if a movie m_6 is added in Table 3.1, with ratings <5, 1, -, 3>, this would mean that expert3 has not yet evaluated this movie. Thus, the dimensional value for movie m_6 corresponding to expert3 is missing. Specifically, in terms of incomplete data, a data point p is said to k-dominate another data point r if there are $k < d$ dimensions in which p is not rated below r or in which at least one of the two points' dimensional values is missing, and is rated higher than r in at least one of these k dimensions (where the dimensional values of p and r are observed). Therefore, on the basis of the k-dominance relationship definition, movie $m6$ is said to 4-dominate movie m_2 across the entire space and to 3-dominate movie m_5 in the $\{expert_1, expert_2, expert_3\}$ subspace.

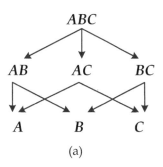

Car	A	B	C
c1	1	60	1
c2	4	50	3
c3	3	30	2
c4	5	40	4
c5	3	40	1

A: price, B: mileage, C: age

Subspace	Skyline
ABC	c1, c3, c5
AB	c1, c3
AC	c1
BC	c3, c5
A	c1
B	c3
C	c1, c5

(a)   (b)   (c)

Figure 3.1: Skycube.

The problem of processing the k-dominant skyline query over incomplete data is systematically studied in Ma et al. (2013) and Miao et al. (2016), who introduce several efficient algorithms.

Finally, Siddique et al. (2015), Ding et al. (2018), and Peng and Chen (2019) present recent developments in k-dominant skyline algorithms which achieve efficiency by exploring data parallelism.

3.2 SKYCUBE

In the skyline analysis context, the *skycube* has been put forward as an optimization which allows users to ask for the non-dominated data points in relation to every selected dimensions set. More precisely, given a d-dimensional dataset, the skycube represents the set of all skylines obtained by this dataset, taking into account every combination of its dimensions, i.e., every possible subspace. In general, a d-dimensional space contains $2^d - 1$ subspaces. A *subspace skyline query* will search for the skyline in one of these $2^d - 1$ subspaces. As shown in Figure 3.1a, taking into account the dimensions A, B, and C, the skycube can be visualized in a lattice structure similar to that of the data cube for a data warehouse. If two cuboids (i.e., subspaces) share some common dimensions and their level differs by one (e.g., cuboids A and AB), the two cuboids are said to have a *child-parent relationship*.

A fitting example for the problem could be the Car dataset of pre-owned cars depicted in Figure 3.1b. The skyline points in relation to the three available attributes A (price, in thousands of euros), B (mileage, in thousands of miles), and C (age, in years) are the cars c_1, c_3, and c_5. The cars c_2 and c_4 are dominated by c_3, for example, because c_3 is cheaper and because it has a lower mileage, and has more recent number plates. A potential buyer who might not consider the price of the car as a determining parameter might, on the other hand, search for the best car in respect of the mileage and the age of the car (i.e., columns B and C). In this case, the skyline points in relation to these two dimensions are only c_3 and c_5. The car c_1 does not represent a skyline point because it is dominated by c_5 (better mileage and same age). By contrast, a potential buyer might only be interested in the price of a car (i.e., column A). In this case, c_1 is the best car. The skycube associated with the Car dataset is the union of the skyline sets in relation to all non-empty subsets (subspaces) of $\{A, B, C\}$, as depicted in Figure 3.1c.

For the skycube to be useful in practical terms, two major directions of research have been taken to date: the first direction has aimed to put forward efficient algorithms for computing the skycube. However, with the number of these skylines rising exponentially in relation to the number of dimensions, both the execution time and storage space costs mean that these solutions struggle with even moderately large datasets and a moderate number (< 10) of dimensions. This drawback has motivated the second direction of researches which has proposed skycube summarization techniques to reduce costs in respect of both time and space.

Pei et al. (2005) and Yuan et al. (2005) were, independently of each other, the first to investigate the problem of d-dimensional subspace skyline analysis. Pei et al. (2005) discussed the subspace skylines primarily from the angle of query semantics. They solved the problem of the skyline membership query, i.e., the problem of why and in which subspaces a data point belongs to the skyline. Yuan et al. (2005) introduced the skycube concept and two algorithms for computing all possible subspace skylines, the BUS (bottom-up skycube) and the TDS (top-down skycube).

The BUS algorithm uses d sorted lists of data points and computes the skycube level by level, from the bottom up. The skyline for every cuboid is computed by a nested-loop based algorithm similar to the SFS algorithm proposed in Chomicki et al. (2005). However to avoid computing every cuboid individually, two computation sharing strategies are introduced. First, during the computation of the skycube, the data points which belong to the skyline sets of the lower level cuboids are added to the skyline set of their (upper level) parent cuboid. This result sharing approach reduces the time needed to compute every skyline set and results in fewer dominance tests since these data points do not need to be re-examined. Second, to avoid an explosion in the number of data sorting processes which the skycube computation requires on the basis of the SFS algorithm, when it computes a cuboid the BUS algorithm uses the sorting produced when the algorithm computed any of its child cuboids. This sorting sharing approach brings about savings in terms of both memory and computation because it reduces the number of data sorting processes required to compute the skycube from $2^d - 1$ to d, i.e., it reduces it to one sorting per dimension. In a top-down fashion, the TDS algorithm uses analogous strategies to take parent cuboids as input and to avoid the need to access the entire dataset multiple times. Thanks to this top-down fashion, TDS is faster than BUS, especially in the case of large or high-dimensional datasets.

Using the same top-down fashion and some sharing strategies on space partitioning, Lee and Hwang (2010) propose a skycube algorithm which is also efficient, called *QSkycube*, which Zhang et al. (2017) later optimized by taking into account more sharing strategies.

Another time-saving approach for query response has been proposed in Bøgh et al. (2014), which puts forward the *HashCube*. This is a bitmap-like index structure which associates a 2^d boolean vector v to every data object p, where the ith position in the vector identifies a subspace. Under this setting, the ith value in the vector is set to TRUE if and only if p belongs to the skyline set of subspace i. While the storage consumption for this method is high, query processing is very fast because retrieving the skyline set for the ith subspace only needs to check the ith position in every vector. The algorithm for constructing the HashCube from scratch is presented in Bøgh et al. (2017).

As already mentioned, because of the exponential number of skylines, some of the research work that has been carried out has aimed to introduce summarization techniques to reduce the execution time and the storage space which the entire skycube occupies. Raïssi et al. (2010) proposed the *closed skycube* concept as a solution which can compress the skycube. The proposed method partitions the $2^d - 1$ cuboids into classes: two cuboids are equivalent if their skyline sets are equal. Hence, the number of skylines is equal to the number of equivalent classes. Once the equivalent classes are identified, the skyline query for every individual cuboid returns the skyline set associated with the equivalence class. However, if the skylines of the subspaces are all different from each other, the size of the closed skycube may reach that of the whole skycube. A second solution is the *Compressed SkyCube*, proposed in Xia et al. (2012). This technique operates at the tuple level on the basis of the realization that a tuple belonging to several skyline sets may not need to be stored in every one of them. The main idea consists in associating a data point p to a subspace X only if X is the smallest subspace for which p belongs in the skyline. Thus, evaluating the skyline query for the subspace X requires first of all that the traversal of all child subspaces of X collects the associated skyline points of these child subspaces before a standard skyline query is executed, to fine-tune the final result. More recently, Alami et al. (2020) explored the notion of the *negative skycube* to find the subspaces in which data points do not belong in the skyline. This research is based on the observation that, to establish whether a data point p is part of the skyline, p should be compared to all the other points in the dataset. However, comparing it to just a single other point r can derive a whole set of subspaces in which p is dominated, i.e., it does not belong to the skylines of these subspaces.

Consider, for example, the Car table depicted in Figure 3.1b, in which cheaper and newer low-mileage cars are preferred. Potential buyers are allowed to search for skylines in relation to any of the $2^3 - 1$ non-empty subsets of $\{A, B, C\}$. A comparison of c_1 and c_5 can reveal that c_1 dominates c_5 in relation to the set of subspaces $s_{15} = \{A, AC\}$. By contrast, and following this comparison, there is no information about the subspaces, in the skylines of which c_5 belongs. Data point c_5 needs to be compared to data point c_3 to discover this (it is noted that no subspace exists in which points c_2 and c_4 dominate c_5, since c_5 dominates both these points across the entire space). Once c_5 is compared to c_3, a new set of subspaces can be derived in which c_5 is dominated, i.e., the set $s_{35} = \{B, AB\}$. Therefore, the subspace $s_{15} \cup s_{35}$ is the set of subspaces where c_5 is dominated. Its complement is the set of subspaces where c_5 is a skyline point, i.e., $\{C, BC, ABC\}$.

However, the storage, for every data point, of the whole set of subspaces where the point does not belong to the skyline might not be feasible in practice because of the large amount of memory space it requires. For this reason, techniques to summarize this set while retaining the efficacy of queries evaluation are also proposed in this last study.

3.3   DYNAMIC SKYLINE QUERIES

The *dynamic skyline query*, introduced by Papadias et al. (2003), is, from a historical point of view, one of the first and possibly the most popular variation of the classical skyline query to appear in the literature. While the algorithms for processing the classical skyline query assume the attributes of the database objects to be static, the algorithms that process the dynamic skyline query either calculate the attributes of the data objects "on-the-fly" in the course of the execution of their algorithmic steps, or calculate them by pre-processing, on the basis of the static attribute values of the objects. A fundamental concept in this query is the *dynamic domination*. On the assumption that lower values are preferable on all the axes (attributes) of the space, a data object p is said to dynamically dominate another object r in relation to a query point q if and only if p is closer to q than r is on at least one axis, while it is not further away from q than r is on all the other axes. Closeness on every axis is measured by calculating the Euclidean distance between the corresponding static attributes of the object and the query point. Therefore, in this domain, rather than being of a static nature, the skyline of a dataset is dynamically generated on the basis of a user's predicate q. In other words, assuming only positive values in all attributes, the classical skyline query can be viewed as a special case of the dynamic skyline query, in which the query point q is located at the origin point of the space.

In comparison to the static skyline, the dynamic skyline offers more flexibility in terms of users specifying their search criteria. More precisely, different users can specify different query points. On the other hand, the very flexibility of the dynamic skyline query brings with it new challenges for efficient query processing. As will be observed in the following sections, the dynamic skyline has served as the foundation block to build several complex skyline and dominance related queries. Taking this query from the perspective of its applicability, it represents a powerful tool in a large number of applications, such as multi-criteria decision-making, business planning, stock market trading, object tracking, the monitoring of the physical environment, location-aware computing, computer games, etc.

In Figure 3.2 the example is of a tourist looking for cheap hotels close to the beach. The query point $q(qx, qy)$ in the figure might represent the preference expressed for a qx euros priced hotel (x-axis) at a qy meters distance from the beach (y-axis). To obtain an "ideal" hotel q, which satisfies the tourist's budget and personal preferences, all eligible hotels that are not dominated by others in relation to q must be retrieved. A skyline analysis will provide recommendations for the best match: every data point p corresponding to a hotel is projected onto a new space, in

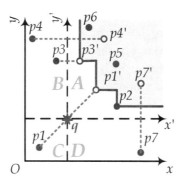

Figure 3.2: Dynamic skyline query.

which the point's coordinate in every dimension equals the absolute difference between the data point p and the query point q. Therefore, the dynamic price of every hotel $p(px, py)$ in relation to $q(qx, qy)$ is calculated as $|px - qx|$, and its dynamic distance is calculated as $|py - qy|$. This actually means that every hotel which is not in quadrant A is mapped into quadrant A in relation to q when calculating the dynamic attributes of the hotel. The figure demonstrates the result. A "static" skyline in the projected space includes the points p_1, p_2, and p_3, which are the hotels that are not dynamically dominated by any other hotel in the dataset in relation to the query predicate q.

Given an indexed dataset using the R-tree, an efficient algorithm for processing the dynamic skyline query is proposed in Papadias et al. (2003) as an extension of the popular BBS algorithm for processing the static skyline query. The only difference which distinguishes it from the BBS algorithm is that the R-tree entries are now inserted into the heap and ordered according to their mindist distance to the query point, which mindist is computed on-the-fly when the entry is considered for the first time (it will be recalled that in the classical BBS algorithm the R-tree entries are inserted in the heap and ordered according to their distance to the origin point of the space). Some other well-known methods for processing the static skyline can also be easily modified to process the dynamic skyline query as well. For example, the straightforward extension of the BNL algorithm, proposed in Börzsönyi et al. (2001) for non-indexed datasets, will evaluate every data point separately after computing all its dynamic coordinates on-the-fly.

Sacharidis et al. (2008) propose a cache-aware algorithm that utilizes the results of the most useful of the past executions of the dynamic skyline query to prune safely parts of the dataset and speed up the execution of any future queries. In addition, to efficiently process the dynamic skyline query over massive data, Han et al. (2019) recently developed a strategy which first retrieves the tuples in dynamic sorted lists in a round-robin fashion until an early termination condition is satisfied, and then computes the dynamic skyline results.

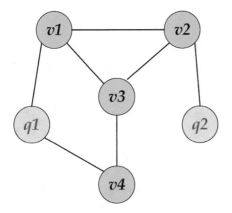

Vertex	d(q1)	d(q2)
v1	1	2
v2	2	1
v3	2	2
v4	1	3

d(q): shortest path distance to q

Figure 3.3: Dynamic skyline query in a graph.

Zou et al. (2010) studied the dynamic skyline operator over large graphs, after extending it from its single-source form to the form of a multi-source query that can deal with more than one query point simultaneously. Given a large edge-weighted graph G and a set Q of query vertices in the graph G, the *dynamic skyline query over a large graph* reports all the vertices in $G - Q$ (i.e., which are not query vertices) that are not dynamically dominated by any other vertex in $G - Q$. As an application example, a social network can be modeled as a large graph in which every vertex corresponds to an individual, and every edge represents the friendship between two corresponding individuals. In this example, an enterprise seeks to establish which salesmen amongst its employees have the "closest" possible relationship with two important potential clients q_1 and q_2. In other terms, the enterprise is looking for the skyline salesmen with respect to these two given potential query points. A salesman v is then a skyline vertex if and only if no other salesman u exists, for which the shortest path distance between u and both q_1 and q_2 is smaller than the shortest path distance of v to these two given query points.

Figure 3.3 considers an undirected graph G and two query vertices q_1 and q_2 in the graph. For the sake of simplicity, all edges are assumed to have the same weight 1. Evidently, in this example, only two skyline vertices exist, and these are v_1 and v_2. The authors employed a filter-and-refine framework to speed up the query processing on the basis of properties of the graph and a specially designed index structure that helps computing the shortest path distances between the vertices of the graph. Recently, Banerjee and Pal (2020) extended the above query to handle the case of uncertain graphs as well.

And, last, a number of recent research efforts, such as those of Zeighami et al. (2020) and Wang et al. (2020b), have introduced frameworks in answer to the need for a secure skyline computation over encrypted datasets for applications in which handling sensitive data is a major issue, such as healthcare or data outsourcing. Setting the problem in this way requires that the main objective for such a framework to be secure relies on finding the dynamic skyline set by processing the data objects in their encrypted form. Such a framework, moreover, needs the shield of strong guarantees that no sensitive information of any kind (either related to the stored data or to the preferences of the query issuer) would be leaked to any third party spying on the data during the execution of the proposed query processing algorithm.

3.4   SPATIAL SKYLINE QUERIES

The *spatial skyline query* is a multi-source extension of the dynamic skyline query, in which every dynamic attribute is calculated as the distance of the data objects to a query point. More specifically, given a set P of data points and a set Q of query points, the spatial skyline query returns those points of P which are not spatially dominated by any other point of P. The *spatial dominance* is established using the distance from the data objects to all query points. Thus, a data point p is said to spatially dominate another point r with respect to Q if and only if $d(p, q_i) \leq d(r, q_i)$ for all $q_i \in Q$ and $d(p, q_j) < d(r, q_j)$ for some $q_j \in Q$, where $d(p, q)$ is the Euclidean distance between p and q.

Spatial skyline queries can apply to a wide range of domains from business planning, crisis management, trip advising to recommender systems, etc. For example, a tourist may prefer the spatial skyline hotels in relation to the fixed locations of a group of interesting attractions. Figure 3.4 illustrates another example where two friends planning to meet up for dinner may wish to select a restaurant from a list. Their final choice will be made on the basis of the distance between every one of these restaurants and their respective homes. Figure 3.4a shows the locations of ten restaurants and the locations $Q = \{q_1, q_2\}$ of the two friends' homes. The restaurants furthest from both of their homes would not qualify. For instance, restaurant p_2 is spatially dominated by restaurant p_1 since both q_1 and q_2 are closer to p_1 than to p_2, as the figure shows. A list of spatial skyline restaurants could be the first step for the two friends toward selecting the restaurant that suits them best. Figure 3.4b shows the distances of all restaurants to q_1 and q_2 in the derived two-dimensional space ($|Q| = 2$). The spatial skyline query will return the $\{p_1, p_3, p_7\}$ set, which is the set of eligible restaurants in relation to the locations q_1 and q_2 of the two friends' homes since, as far as the remaining restaurants are concerned, the two friends would have to travel a longer distance starting from their homes q_1 and q_2 to meet up.

Sharifzadeh and Shahabi (2006) were the first to study the problem of spatial skyline query analysis. They proposed two index-based algorithms to efficiently process this query: the B^2S^2 (branch and bound spatial skyline) algorithm and the VS^2 (Voronoi-based spatial skyline) algorithm. B^2S^2 searches for spatial skyline candidate points by visiting the traditional R-tree spatial index from top to bottom. Once a spatial skyline point is found, B^2S^2 expands the R-tree to access the node with the minimum mindist distance value to that data point and checks the dominance between the visited node and all the spatial skyline candidate points found so far.

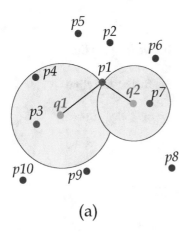
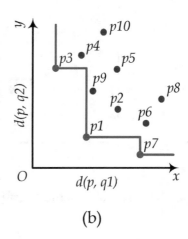

(a)   (b)

Figure 3.4: Spatial skyline query.

On the other hand, the VS^2 algorithm relies on a Voronoi diagram created using the input data points. The input data points are organized in disk pages according to their Hilbert values to preserve their locality. Upon the completion of the convex hull calculation, VS^2 starts with the closest data points to the query points and searches the space by visiting the neighbors of the already visited data points using the Voronoi diagram. For every visited data point, VS^2 carries out a comparison with all the spatial skylines found so far to establish spatial dominance. The process continues until all Voronoi cells (or data points) that potentially contain spatial skyline points have been visited. To deal with the high computational cost involved, VS^2 was improved in Son et al. (2009) by reducing the number of the spatial dominance tests performed.

The above methods study the spatial skyline query by using the Euclidean (or L_2) distance, which, however, lacks in efficiency in application domains which involve constraint-based environments of residential blocks or road networks. A method for computing the spatial skyline in a grid network especially aimed at urban residential areas, for example, using the Manhattan (or L_1) distance, has been put forward in Son et al. (2014). Deng et al. (2007), on the other hand, investigated the spatial skyline query problem in road networks. In this setting, the Euclidean distance between the data and query points is replaced by the shortest path distance between them. Given a set P of data objects and a set Q of query points on a road network, every data object is mapped onto a $|Q|$-dimensional point, where the value of its ith dimension refers to the shortest path between the object and the ith query point. The *multi-source skyline query* then retrieves the data objects that are not dominated in terms of the $|Q|$ dimensions of this space. Another solution for the same problem is presented in Safar et al. (2011).

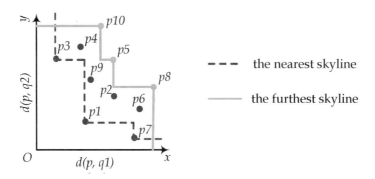

Figure 3.5: Nearest and the farthest spatial skyline queries.

As concerns the opposite goal, that is the identification of eligible points that are the furthest from location query points, You et al. (2013) introduce the *farthest spatial skyline query*, which retrieves the data points that are farther than all the other data points from the query points. This query also serves a wide range of application, such as supporting decision-making processes, the planning of trips and events, locating facilities, crisis management, etc. The query can help to identify the most desirable spatial locations far away from other undesirable locations. A few examples would be when a location is sought for the establishment of a new franchise store which has to be the furthest away possible from the locations of the branches of competing franchises or when a location is sought for the establishment of a new school which has to be the furthest away possible from the locations of sites which could have potentially detrimental effects on the well-being of the school-children and or/and on the functioning of the school. Figure 3.4a already seen above illustrates an example of a set of ten restaurants and of the home locations q_1 and q_2 of two friends who wish to select a restaurant on the basis of the distance between their two homes and the potential restaurants. As Figure 3.4b has shown, the most convenient choice of restaurants for easy access from the two friends' homes are the nearest spatial skyline restaurants p_1, p_3, and p_7. If, however, Figure 3.4a is assumed to illustrate a set of ten potential locations that are required to build a new school and there are two locations q_1 and q_2 which represent, respectively, a chemical plant and a garbage dump, Figure 3.5 then indicates that the most eligible locations for the new school, that are furthest away from these two undesirable sites, are the farthest spatial skyline locations p_5, p_8, and p_{10}. The same problem is also studied in Fort et al. (2020).

In addition, Kodama et al. (2009) uses the spatial skyline query to recommend objects, such as restaurants, to a mobile user (a single query point), by taking into account the user's current location and preferences. Here, the user's preferences are represented by the non-spatial attributes of the objects. Thus, this solution integrates non-spatial attributes into the spatial sky-

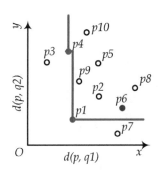

Restaurant	textual descriptions
p1	healthy, sups, seafood, informal, relaxed
p2	takeout, cheap, fast food, cafe
p3	romantic, fine dining, gluten free
p4	sups, seafood, vegan, relaxed, informal
p5	TV, Italian, pizza, relaxed
p6	seafood, sups, desert, informal, relaxed
p7	WiFi, Greek, seafood, scenic view
p8	sups, meat, desert, informal
p9	buffet, live music, parking available
p10	drive thru, sups, grill, seafood

Figure 3.6: Spatio-textual skyline query.

line query and, for this reason, its applications range is very wide, from recommending locations or sites, to planning trips and advertising.

Shi et al. (2015) put forward an extension of the above problem so that the query, called *spatio-textual skyline query* in their paper, considers multiple query points. Therefore, the skyline points in this query can be selected on the basis of both their distance to a set of query locations and their relevance to a set of query keywords. The query is especially adapted to modern applications, where it has become the norm for preferences to be augmented with textual descriptions. By recalling again Figure 3.4a which considers two friends looking for potential restaurants that are not far from their homes q_1 and q_2, it can be additionally assumed that they prefer restaurants offering "sups" and "seafood" on the menu, an "informal" environment and "relaxed" atmosphere. Figure 3.6 illustrates the inclusion of the textual descriptions for the ten available restaurants. As Figure 3.4b has shown, the conventional spatial query result for this example is the set of restaurants $\{p_1, p_3, p_7\}$. However, after taking the textual preferences of the two friends into consideration, as Figure 3.6 illustrates, the most eligible restaurants are now the p_1, p_4, and p_6, out of which only p_1 and p_4 belong in the spatio-textual skyline since p_6 is spatially dominated by p_1 which is closer to both q_1 and q_2.

Another method that also considers a single query point is presented in Guo et al. (2010), which introduce the *direction-based spatial skyline query* that retrieves nearest points around a mobile user (a single query point) by taking into consideration not only the distance between these points and the mobile user but also the direction. Figure 3.7 depicts eight target points of interest around the query point q which represents the user's location. The vectors $\vec{p}_1$ to $\vec{p}_8$ in the figure originate from q. Two vectors are considered to be in the same direction if the angle between them is smaller than a specified acceptable threshold, for example, less than

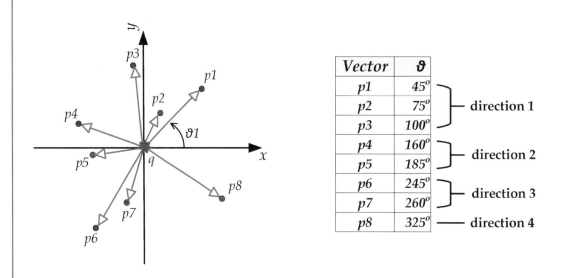

Vector	ϑ	
p1	45°	direction 1
p2	75°	
p3	100°	
p4	160°	direction 2
p5	185°	
p6	245°	direction 3
p7	260°	
p8	325°	direction 4

Figure 3.7: Direction-based spatial skyline query.

$60°$. This means that the data points which are in the same direction as the data point p_1 are the data points p_2 and p_3. Since, out of p_1, p_2, and p_3, p_2 is the closest point to q, it is said that p_2 dominates the other two data points in the same direction and represents one of the points to be recommended to the user. In a similar way, p_5 dominates p_4; p_7 dominates p_6; and finally p_8 has no other comparable data point in the same direction. Thus, p_2, p_5, p_7, and p_8 are not dominated by any other object and, consequently, they constitute the direction-based spatial skyline in relation to q. A real-life example might be the case of a mobile user who has not decided yet which direction to take and seeks a recommendation system to find the nearest restaurants in every potential direction. The solution proposed by Guo et al. (2010) for direction-based spatial skyline analysis also supports continuous queries for cases in which the user is moving linearly.

Following a thorough examination of the above work, Shen et al. (2020) concluded that it presented issues that burdened its efficiency which could not be overlooked. For example, if a small acceptance threshold is set (such as $10°$) so that the angle between two data points means that these two points are considered to belong in the same direction, Guo et al.'s above method might return too many data points (hence, the too many answers problem). If, on the contrary, the acceptance threshold angle increases to larger values (such as $60°$), only a few data objects will be included in the direction-based spatial skyline (hence, the too few answers problem), which is also unsatisfactory in terms of retrieving a sufficient selection of surrounding data objects for the user. The authors in Shen et al. (2020) addressed these drawbacks by putting forward a new solution, which is both more flexible and robust in retrieving the most eligible surrounding points under the direction-based spatial skyline problem. In addition, Shen et al. (2019) proposed for the same query problem algorithms that can handle and retrieve arbitrary-shaped non-dominated surrounding data objects in relation to the user's location.

And last, Wang et al. (2017b) observed that with the rapid growth of spatial data, addressing the spatial skyline query on large-scale spatial datasets using a single processing node becomes impractical. For this reason, they introduced an advanced MapReduce-based parallel framework to address the conventional spatial skyline query on large-scale datasets. The approach first calculates the convex hull of the query points. The authors then propose the concept of independent regions whereby the input data points are partitioned according to their associated independent regions. Finally, the local spatial skyline in every independent region is calculated simultaneously, and the global spatial skyline is constructed on the basis of the union of all the local spatial skyline sets.

3.5 METRIC SPACE SKYLINE QUERIES

As discussed in the previous section, given a set of data objects and a set of query points, the spatial skyline query relies on the dynamic calculation of the Euclidean distances of every object from every query point. Using these distances as dynamic attributes, every object is then transformed into a vector in a new multi-dimensional space, in which the number of dimensions equals the number of query points. Classically, the skyline operator then selects the data objects for which no other object exists that has a smaller or an equal Euclidean distance to all the query points.

Taking this definition of the spatial skyline query as a stepping stone, Chen and Lian (2009) introduce the *metric skyline query*, in which the dynamic attributes of every data object are calculated on the basis of a set of dimension functions. This means that the spatial and the metric skyline queries mainly differ on account of the fact that the distance functions used in the metric skyline query consists not only of the Euclidean distance function but also of other types of metric functions. In contrast to the spatial skyline query, the metric skyline query is therefore a more generic type of query and it is not restricted to spatial data application domains in which the objects can be represented in the form of vectors in the Euclidean space.

For example, to deal with an image similarity search, more than one query image might be used to increase the accuracy of the search, such as those images that can be extracted out of a scene from a video sequence or the images that can be extracted from the footage of a scene taken from several security cameras. In this example of the applicability of the metric skyline query, the images can be mapped out as points onto a metric space in which the similarity between any two images can be measured for instance on the basis of the Hausdorff distance (Huttenlocher et al., 1993). Therefore, an image p dominates another image r in relation to a given set of query images, if p is more (or equally) similar to all query images than r is. The metric skyline query should then retrieve the images in the database which are not dominated by any other image in relation to the given set of query images.

In another real-life example, following the discovery and verification of the user's profiles (query points) that a targeted entity of the physical world maintains in a number of online social networks, the database of the user profiles (data points) in another online social network can be attacked on the basis of the metric skyline query to find the potentially eligible profiles, one of which might be the profile of that same physical world entity in this other online social network. This is an example of the problem of linking multiple social identities across heterogeneous on-line social networks. The distance-based comparison between any two such user profiles in this problem can be carried out using a mixed function which will calculate the overall weighted similarity score of both the corresponding text-based personal attributes of the two profiles (e.g., using a text similarity comparison metric such as one of those surveyed in Elmagarmid et al. (2006)), and the profile images—if they exist—in the two separate profiles (e.g., using the Hausdorff comparison metric), following, for example, a profile correlation model analogous to that proposed in Kokkos et al. (2017).

It is important to keep in mind the fact that skyline query processing in a metric space cannot make use of any geometric information to guide the pruning. This means that methods such as the approach that retrieves the spatial skyline in the Euclidean space are inapplicable to the generic metric skyline scenarios. Taking the case of any three points p, r, and q in the metric space, the distance function $d()$ used in the metric skyline query would need, however, to satisfy the following four properties: (i) positivity: $d(p, q) \geq 0$; (ii) identity: $d(p, r) = 0 \iff p = r$; (iii) symmetry: $d(p, q) = d(q, p)$; and (iv) triangle inequality: $d(p, r) \leq d(p, q) + d(q, r)$. These properties are therefore the only available tools to facilitate the metric skyline search.

The authors who introduced the metric skyline query in Chen and Lian (2009) process the query via indices in the metric space. These indices can significantly reduce the search space by filtering out the unqualified data objects as early as possible. More specifically, the proposed method uses the M-tree, a dynamic multi-dimensional access method for data objects in a metric space, introduced in Skopal (2004). The M-tree selects some data objects to serve as centers (i.e., local pivots) of hyper-spheres, and the remaining objects are divided up between these hyper-spheres to build up a balanced and compact hierarchy. Figure 3.8 depicts a small M-tree in a two-dimensional metric space that contains ten data points $p_1, p_2, \ldots,$ and p_{10} and the minimum bounding circles $e_0, e_1, \ldots,$ and e_6 that have been built on top of these data objects, with e_0 as the root of the M-tree. For the sake of presentation the example uses the Euclidean distance as the similarity measure. The example assumes the existence of two query points q_1 and q_2.

Upon the construction of the M-tree, the method searches the index for metric skyline points in a best-first manner (by traversing the tree, starting from its root) using the traditional BBS algorithm proposed in Papadias et al. (2003). The first step consists in the algorithm accessing the root e_0 of the tree and inserting its descendant nodes e_1 and e_2 into an auxiliary heap

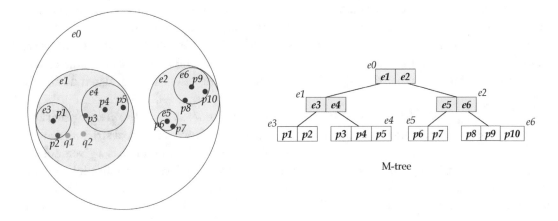

Figure 3.8: Metric skyline query.

in the form of (*entry*, *key*), where *key* is the sum of the minimum distances of the entry (e.g., e_1) and every query point. Since q_1 and q_2 are positioned in the cycle of e_1, the entry e_1 is extracted first from the heap and its descendant nodes e_3 and e_4 are inserted into the heap. Subsequently, e_3 is popped from the heap and its data entries p_1 and p_2 are added back to the heap. Following this, p_2 is popped from the heap, since this data point has the smaller sum of metric distances to q_1 and q_2, and it is therefore inserted in the metric skyline set. Then e_4 is popped from the heap and its data entries p_3, p_4, and p_5 return to the heap. Then p_3 is popped from the heap and, since among all the available data entries it has the smaller metric distance to q_2, it is also added to the metric skyline set. Following the same technique, in the next step the data entry p_1 is extracted from the heap, the attribute vector of which is dominated by that of p_2 and therefore p_1 is discarded. At the end of the process, which is executed exactly along the same steps as in the traditional BBS algorithm, the metric skyline set is comprised of the points p_2 and p_3. Thus, the main advantage in using the M-tree and the BBS algorithm is that with this method some branches of the tree can be filtered away and therefore the (usually) "expensive" computation of the metric distance functions between the query points and a large part of the dataset can be avoided.

The method for processing the metric skyline query proposed by Skopal and Lokoc (2010) shares some characteristics with the method proposed in Chen and Lian (2009). The main difference is that in the latter method the M-tree is replaced by the PM-tree (Skopal, 2004), which is also an efficient metric access method. It operates by further cutting off the original hyperspheres of the M-tree by means of a set of hyper-rings (again centered by pivots), so that the region volume of every tree node can become more compact.

Fuhry et al. (2009), in addition, discovered some significant relationships in the metric space between the skyline query and other popular similarity queries, such as the nearest neighbor and the range queries. The authors developed techniques relying on these relationships to aggressively prune non-skyline points from the search space. On the basis of this discovery, the authors proposed optimized algorithms which reduce both the number of dominance tests and the number of times that the expensive metric distance functions are calculated during the process.

Last, Jiang et al. (2015) introduced the *top–k combinatorial metric skyline query*, which aims to find the best k combinations of data points on a metric space according to a strict monotonic preference function, so that every one of these combinations of data points has a given point p in its metric skyline. This query is particularly adapted to facility location applications such as the case of an enterprise in the process of selecting locations for two new franchise stores in the proximity of an existing warehouse p. These locations can be selected out of several available eligible locations. To avoid wasteful competitions between branches of the same company and to reach new customers, neither of these two new locations should be in the proximity of any other of their existing stores. To follow a location strategy of this kind, the combinations of the two locations should have point p at their metric skyline. It is worth observing that all the algorithms mentioned earlier in this section have focused exclusively on the individual data objects, and not on combinations of data objects and cannot, therefore, be applied to solve this particular problem.

In conclusion, it would appear that in the metric skyline query context (as well as in the spatial skyline query context discussed in the previous section) the number of query points that is used in a query represents an important parameter which needs appropriate fine-tuning in every application. If only one query point is used, the metric skyline query turns into the classical 1-nearest neighbor query. If, on the other hand, the number of query points multiples, the size of the skyline is likely to grow substantially and, in this way, would end up being of little or no use to the query issuer. Therefore, to provide a result that is sufficiently discriminating to be of value to the query issuer, the metric skyline query should start from a small number of query points, for example no more than five query points, depending on the problem that needs solving.

3.6   RANGE-BASED SKYLINE QUERIES

The *range skyline* search is a preference-oriented type of query which combines the properties of the traditional range query and the point-based skyline query. Therefore, as expected, none of the existing point-based skyline search algorithms is applicable to this query. Papadias et al. (2003) introduced the *constrained skyline query* whereby the results of the traditional skyline query include only the most interesting data points with coordinate values within a specified range. In the example of Figure 3.9, a tourist might look for cheap hotels close to the beach. The traditional (static) skyline query retrieves the interesting hotels that are not dominated by others in relation to the space origin point $O = (0,0)$, i.e., the data points p_1, p_3, and p_7. However, if the

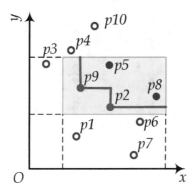

Figure 3.9: Constrained skyline query.

query issuer is interested only in hotels with prices (x-axis) in the range [50, 100] and distances to the sea (y-axis) in the range [200, 500], the "local" skyline in the specified two-dimensional range will contain the points p_2 and p_9, which correspond to the most interesting hotels with attribute values in that range. Chen et al. (2011) extended this work to deal with cases in which the relevant data are distributed among geographically scattered sites in unstructured distributed environments.

In the meantime, Huang et al. (2006b) proposed the continuous monitoring of the traditional point-based skyline, whereby both the query point and the data points can continuously shift along a line at a constant speed in every dimension. Their proposed solution does not need to compute the skyline from scratch at every time instance. Instead, the possible change from one time to another is predicted, thus making sure the skyline query result is updated and continuously available. The approach can be particularly useful in real-time applications such as computer games and digital war systems, for instance when a player in a field-fighting game wishes to keep track of those enemies in motion who are close and most dangerous in multiple respects simultaneously (energy, weaponry, strategy, etc.).

In addition, Lai et al. (2016) focus on the distributed domain over mobile wireless sensor networks in which only the data points within a given maximum distance (radius) of the query point q can be candidates for the traditional point-based skyline query. In the first step of the proposed method the query node q spreads the range-based skyline query to its neighbor nodes. Then, the neighbors of q use their own local data to derive their local range-skyline results and return them to the query node q. Once q has received the local range-skyline results from its neighbors, it checks the dominance relations between all the candidate data points and derives the final range-skyline set. Later on, Lai et al. (2019a) extend their approach to take node mo-

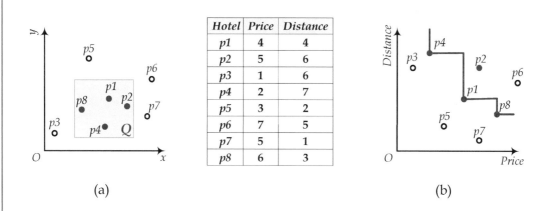

Hotel	Price	Distance
p1	4	4
p2	5	6
p3	1	6
p4	2	7
p5	3	2
p6	7	5
p7	5	1
p8	6	3

(a)　　　　　　　　　　　　　　　　　　　　　(b)

Figure 3.10: Type of range-skyline query proposed in Rahul and Janardan (2012).

bility into account because the movement of the sensor nodes may cause the answer to change frequently.

Rahul and Janardan (2012) proposed a method for the retrieval of the local skyline of all the data points lying within a small neighborhood of interest, specified as a query region on the xy-plane. In Figure 3.10a, a set of eight hotels in the xy-plane is shown. The hotels p_1, p_2, p_4, and p_8 (shown filled) lie in the query rectangle Q. The static local skyline of these four hotels is to be computed in relation to the information regarding price and distance to the beach shown in the table. In Figure 3.10b, the skyline points p_1, p_4, and p_8 are highlighted.

In a more general case of this problem, the authors divide the space in s dimensions that represent the coordinates of the data points and in t dimensions that represent the features of the data points and which are used to find those data points that are the most eligible on the basis of the traditional skyline search. The skyline set thus consists of those points in the dataset that belong in a specific range of values in the first s of their attributes and that are not dominated by any other point in relation to the last t of their attributes.

Since the confidentiality of a user's preferences and location has become an important issue, *privacy-preserving range-based skyline queries* have been incorporated into mobile applications. Lin et al. (2013) model the approximate location of the query issuer on the 2-dimensional space as a range and they compute the skyline after defining the domination relation between two data points on the basis of both their distance to the blurred range-based location of the user and the monotonic order in any other available attribute. For example, in Figure 3.11a the rectangle Q represents the input range of the query (e.g., the blurred location of a tourist) and the points $p_1, p_2, \ldots$, and p_6 represent the locations of six hotels. The non-spatial attributes of the hotels are shown in Figure 3.11b. Given two hotels p and r, if p is no worse than r in the

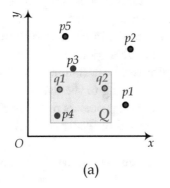

Hotel	Price	Distance
p1	4	4
p2	5	6
p3	1	2
p4	3	7
p5	3	2

(a)   (b)

Figure 3.11: Privacy-preserving range-based skyline query.

non-spatial attributes and if p is closer than r to the query range, then p dominates r. A skyline query's purpose is to find all hotels that are not dominated by any other hotel. Thus, the skyline results depend on the location of the query issuer. For example, if the query issuer is located on point q_1, the skyline result set is only comprised of hotel p_3 because this hotel is both cheaper and closer to the beach than all the other hotels, while it is at the same time closer to the location q_1 of the query issuer. If, however, the query point is q_2, the skyline result set is comprised of hotels p_1 and p_3, because all the other hotels are dominated by p_3, while p_2 is also dominated by p_1. Thus, such a range-based skyline query should return a collective set of skyline results for every possible query point in Q.

Since the above approach considers only the Euclidean space, Fu et al. (2017) extended it to consider objects moving on the space of a road network. This privacy-preserving range-based skyline query also takes as input the spatial range Q of the user's blurred location. However, in this case, the domination relationship between these data objects is defined on the basis of the objects' non-spatial attributes and on the basis of their shortest path distance to every possible query point q of the user's location. The authors also consider the case in which the user and the data objects move with time on the road network.

Wang et al. (2011b) were the first to propose an algorithm for dynamic skyline query processing by considering the query as a range in every dimension rather than as a point. Given the query range, a data point can be in the range skyline only if it is not dynamically dominated by any other data point in relation to every query point in the given range. The method uses a grid index and a variant of the well-known Z-order curve to prune the vast majority of data points which cannot be part of the dynamic skyline and the final range skyline set can be retrieved using a non-index skyline processing algorithm, such as the SFS algorithm proposed in Chomicki et al. (2005).

Finally, Tzouramanis et al. (2018) focus on a more general case and take the above work further in several directions. First, their approach considers that a data point can be in the range skyline if it is not dynamically dominated by any other data point in relation to any individual query point in the d-dimensional range, i.e., not necessarily in relation to all the query points in the range. Second, their proposed solution defines the sub-region (of the given range) in relation to which a data point can belong to the range skyline set. Last, their approach uses a traditional spatial index to prune all the data points that do not belong to the dynamic skyline in relation to the given range, with no need to implement additional processes or to use non-index skyline processing algorithms to remove false hits as the method of Wang et al. (2011b) is obliged to do.

These adjustments greatly extend the application domains in which the range skyline query concept can be adopted. For example, a tourist might be interested in posting a query targeting an interval of "ideal" values on every dimension, instead of a precise value, e.g., targeting the best hotels charging between 50 and 100 euros per night and located at a distance from the beach of between 200 and 500 meters. Any hotel belonging to the dynamic skyline in relation to any query point (and not necessarily in relation to all the query points) in the given range might be eligible. This solution is also particularly useful in privacy preservation domains in which the user preferences for executing the dynamic skyline query can be expressed using an interval of values on every dimension instead of precise values, thus producing a d-dimensional hyper-rectangle query pattern, rather than a point query. For instance, the user might be asked to provide confidential information (e.g., blood pressure, etc.) in a service offering customized fitness and health advice. In such a context the user might feel more comfortable submitting this personal information in an opaque manner. Figure 3.12 illustrates a two-dimensional rectangular range Q in relation to which the user might search for the range skyline of a given dataset. For the sake of illustration, the figure also shows the point-based dynamic skyline in relation to two of the infinite points in Q, i.e., Figure 3.12a shows the point-based dynamic skyline in relation to the lower-left corner q_1 of Q and Figure 3.12b shows the point-based dynamic skyline in relation to the upper-right corner q_2 of Q. As the figures illustrate, the data point p_1 appears in both these two skyline sets and it can be shown that this data point is actually the only one that is not dynamically dominated by any other data point in relation to every query point in the range. Therefore p_1 is the only data point that will be returned by the method put forward by Wang et al. (2011b) discussed above. In addition, the points p_2, p_3, p_4, and p_5 belong to the range skyline set only in relation to a specific sub-region of Q.

3.7   OTHER VARIATIONS

In this broad area of research, the sheer volume of publications on the generalization and extension of the basic framework of the skyline query for handling different types of data and application domains makes it too difficult to cover in this chapter the multitude of issues that

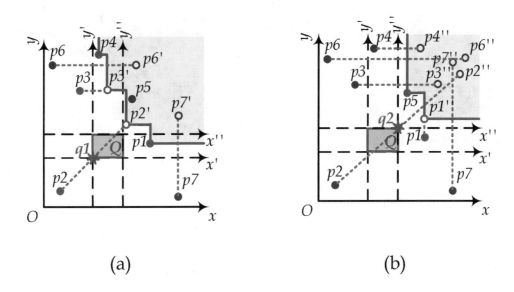

(a)   (b)

Figure 3.12: Range skyline query.

have been raised and studied until now. The many research contributions that it has been practically impossible to cover, include, to mention but a few, the variations illustrated in Table 3.2.
    For example, the *fuzzy dominance skyline query* selects and discriminates tuples that are ac-
tually not dominated and also tuples that are dominated but only just. The *k most representative
skyline query* selects *k* skyline data objects so that the total number of data objects which are dominated by at least one of these *k* skyline data objects is maximized. The *k-skyband query* returns
the data points that are not dominated by more than *k* other data points. Hence, the parameter
k specifies the width of a skyband query result sought by the user. The *reverse skyline query* finds
all the data points that have a given query point *q* as a member of their dynamic skylines. The
skyline query on categorical data (or categorical skyline) finds out the most eligible data objects
in applications in which the attributes of the data objects are drawn from low-cardinality, or
from categorical or boolean-valued domains. The *temporal skyline query* considers the period of
validity or existence of the data and of the query objects, for example simulating hotels opening
exclusively in the summer. The *thick* and the *σ-neighborhood skyline queries* recommend not only
skyline data objects but also their nearby neighbors within a predefined threshold distance. The
top-k ranked skyline query finds the *k* skyline points which dominate the largest number of data
points, where *k* is again a query parameter. For a given data point, the *why-not skyline query* aims
at providing (i) an explanation which accounts for the reason why this point is not in the answer

Table 3.2: Other variations of skyline and other dominance-based queries (*Continues.*)

Query Variation	References
Approximate skyline query	Koltun and Papadimitriou (2007), Yin et al. (2019), etc.
Enumerating skyline query	Papadias et al. (2003), etc.
Fuzzy dominance skyline query	Goncalves and Tineo (2007), etc.
Group-based (G-) skyline query	Liu et al. (2015), Wang et al. (2017a), Zhou et al. (2020), etc.
Group-by skyline query	Luk et al. (2009), Wang et al. (2016b), etc.
k most representative skyline query	Lin et al. (2007), Tao et al. (2009), Sarma et al. (2011), etc.
k-skyband query	Papadias et al. (2003), Gao et al. (2014b), etc.
Mutual skyline query	Jiang et al. (2014), etc.
Parallel skyline query	Gao et al. (2006), Köhler et al. (2011), Afrati et al. (2015), etc.
Prioritized skyline query	Mindolin and Chomicki (2011), etc.
Probabilistic (P-) skyline query	Jiang et al. (2012), Zhang et al. (2013), etc.
Ranked skyline query	Papadias et al. (2003), etc.
Reverse skyline query	Dellis and Seeger (2007), Lian and Chen (2008a), Lian and Chen (2008b), Wang et al. (2011a), Gao et al. (2014a), Lim et al. (2019), etc.
SkyCluster query	Huang et al. (2011), etc.
Skyline query on aggregate data	Magnani and Assent (2013), etc.
Skyline query on categorical data	Morse et al. (2007b), Sarkas et al. (2008), Rahman et al. (2017)
Skyline query on time series	Jiang and Pei (2009), He et al. (2016), etc.
Skyline query over joins	Jin et al. (2010), Vlachou et al. (2011), Khalefa et al. (2011), Raghavan et al. (2011), Yin et al. (2020), etc.
Skyline query over sliding windows	Lin et al. (2005), Zhang et al. (2009b) etc.
Skyline query with trade-offs	Lofi et al. (2010), etc.
Skyline on partially ordered domains	Chan et al. (2005), Sacharidis et al. (2009), etc.
Stochastic skyline query	Zhang et al. (2012), etc.
Temporal skyline query	Kalyvas et al. (2017), etc.

Table 3.2: (*Continued.*) Other variations of skyline and other dominance-based queries

Thick and σ-neighborhood skyline queries	Jin et al. (2004), Chen and Lee (2015), etc.
Top-k skyline query	Lee et al. (2009), etc.
Uncertain (U-) skyline query	Liu et al. (2012), etc.
Why-not skyline query	Islam et al. (2013), Miao et al. (2018), Sun et al. (2020), etc.

set of the query and (ii) the answer about which is the optimal modification solution with the minimal penalty so that this point will be included in the results set.

Together with the query variations of skyline and other dominance-based queries which have been discussed in more detail in the previous sections of this chapter, the scope and diversity of the types of query variants that have only been briefly mentioned for the sake of reference in the present section bear witness to the prominence and visibility, as well as to the enduring vitality and the abundance of the research on skyline and other dominance-based queries. In this light, in view of the proliferation of skyline query variants, Zhang et al. (2010b) have proposed a particularly interesting generalized framework to guide the extension of the classical skyline problem from its conventional definition to its different variants from the databases perspective. The study also provides some insights into properties of the dominance relationship that should be preserved in a query variation so that it will maintain its original advantages, and also some insights into properties of the dominance relationship that can be relaxed so that the query might extend its adaptive qualities to application semantics, while keeping its computational complexity to a minimum.

3.8   SUMMARY

The skyline query has drawn attention because the extent to which its essential quality in articulating requests for information supports effective retrieval over massive multidimensional data. However, its success does not stretch to handling a number of applications, the nature and complexity of which have created a demand for modifications and extensions of the traditional skyline definition. Having perceived this need, several research teams have contributed new variants to the classical skyline problem over the last two decades, as well as algorithms to process these variants efficiently in relational databases.

This chapter has focused on the k-dominant skyline queries, skycube, dynamic skyline queries, spatial skyline queries, metric skyline queries, and range-based skyline queries, as some of the most representative families of extensions of the traditional skyline query in the databases domain. These queries have also received a great deal of attention because of their enhanced ability to relate to present-day requirements and because they represent an approach applicable in a more attuned way to a wide range of domains, such as in multi-preference analysis and decision-making support, business planning, stock market trading, advertisement, healthcare, molecular biology, geographic information systems, location-aware computing, trip advising and events planning, facility location and place recommendation, traffic networks, physical environment monitoring, crisis management, e-games, etc. The awareness of the need for more advanced approaches which is reflected in these exciting new queries, as well as the significant breakthroughs which they represent, means that there is a bright future ahead. Many avenues of research lies ahead and will focus either on further boosting the performance of existing query processing algorithms (e.g., by improving their pruning power or their computational speed) or on exploring new promising queries in/or other emerging domains requiring preference-based computation.

The next chapter is dedicated to the top-k dominating queries, a family of significant variations of the traditional skyline analysis problem. The main aim of these queries is to tackle the Achilles' heel of the skyline query, which is the lack of a systematic internal mechanism able to control the number of skyline points being returned, i.e., the size of the skyline set which sometimes might be impractically over-sized and sometimes inconveniently under-sized. Because of this all-important quality and of its capacity to guarantee a robust query result, among the various extensions of the skyline query the top-k dominating queries family has attracted some of the keenest research interest. The chapter will study the top-k dominating queries analysis under a variety of settings and perspectives to highlight its great flexibility and its expanding applicability.

CHAPTER 4

Top-*k* Dominating Queries

This chapter presents the top-*k* dominating query with examples and several algorithms and solutions that have been proposed for efficient query processing. Top-*k* dominating queries have been studied by different perspectives, such as in indexed and non-indexed multi-dimensional data using efficient exact computation algorithms, in uncertain data using randomized algorithms with accuracy guarantees, and in data streams. Moreover, top-*k* dominating queries have been studied over distance-based dynamic attribute vectors, defined over a metric space, using efficient progressive algorithms. Top-*k* dominating queries have become an important tool for decision support, data mining, Web search, and multi-criteria retrieval applications.

4.1   PROBLEM DEFINITION

The most important advantage of a top-*k* query is that the number of results is bounded (which is not true for skyline queries), whereas the most important advantage of a skyline query is that no parameters and user-defined scoring functions are required.

A top-*k* dominating query combines the advantages of a top-*k* query and a skyline query, and avoids their disadvantages by assigning to each object an intuitive score based on dominance. It returns *k* objects with the highest domination scores (i.e., the number of dominated objects). This score is reflecting the importance of every object in the dataset in a natural way. As a top-*k* query, the user can bound the number of returned results through the parameter *k*, and as a skyline query a user-selected scoring function is not required.

More formally, in case of multi-dimensional data, let P bes a dataset with d-dimensional objects. The object $p = (p \cdot x_1, p \cdot x_2, \ldots, p \cdot x_d) \in P$ *dominates* another object $q = (q \cdot x_1, q \cdot x_2, \ldots, q \cdot x_d) \in D$, i.e., $p \prec q$, when: $\forall i \in \{1, \ldots, d\} : p \cdot x_i \leq q \cdot x_i \wedge \exists i \in \{1, \ldots, d\} : p \cdot x_i < q \cdot x_i$ (without loss of generality, we assume that there is preference in small values in all dimensions). This means that p is as good as q in all dimensions, and it is strictly better than q in at least one dimension. The domination score of p, $dom(p)$ is defined as: $dom(p) = |\{q \in D : p \prec q\}|$. A top-*k* dominating query returns the *k* objects with the maximum domination scores.

Figure 4.1 depicts an example. There are 15 objects that are two-dimensional points (p_i, for $i=1,\ldots,15$). The domination region of a point p_i contains all points that p_i dominates. By using domination regions, we can calculate all domination scores of the points p_i, i.e., $dom(p_1) = 0$, $dom(p_2) = 0$, $dom(p_3) = 1$, $dom(p_4) = 0$, $dom(p_5) = 1$, $dom(p_6) = 5$, $dom(p_7) = 5$, $dom(p_8) = 1$, $dom(p_9) = 6$, $dom(p_{10}) = 4$, $dom(p_{11}) = 10$, $dom(p_{12}) = 1$,

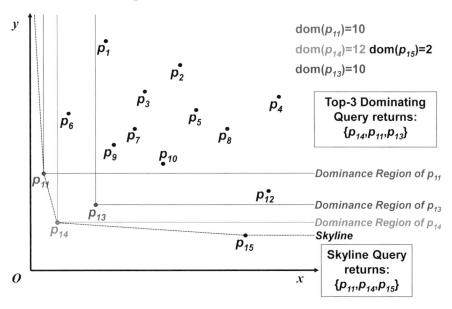

Figure 4.1: Top-3 dominating query.

$dom(p_{13}) = 10$, $dom(p_{14}) = 12$, $dom(p_{15}) = 2$. Therefore, a top-3 dominating query must return the points p_{14}, p_{11}, p_{13}. It is interesting that p_{11} and p_{14} are skyline points, but p_{13} is not.

4.2   A SKYLINE-BASED ALGORITHM

The first approach for processing top-*k* dominating queries has been presented in Papadias et al. (2005a), where the top-*k* dominating query has been defined as a variation of the skyline query. A Skyline-Based Top-*k* Dominating Algorithm (STD) has been proposed, which uses the Branch-and-Bound Skyline Algorithm (BBS) of Papadias et al. (2005a). The main steps taken by STD are the following.

- Compute the skyline *SKY*(*P*) of the dataset *P*.

- For each object $p \in SKY(P)$ count the number of objects it dominates (i.e., its score $dom(p)$).

- Sort the objects in *SKY*(*P*) by their domination scores and report the object *q* with the maximum domination score (top-1). The domination scores are kept in a sorted list *L*.

- Then, the *exclusive domination region R* of *q* is selected and a local skyline query constrained in *R* is performed. The exclusive domination region of an object *q* of *SKY*(*P*)

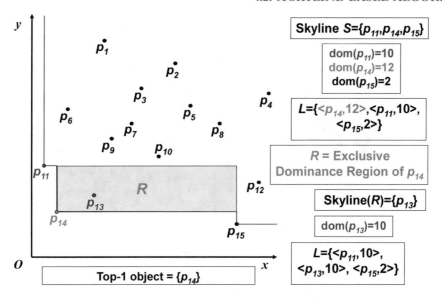

Figure 4.2: First iteration of STD algorithm.

is the region which contains the objects dominated only by q and not by any other object of the skyline $SKY(P)$. After the execution of the constrained skyline query in R, q is removed.

- The domination values of all skyline objects in R are computed and the sorted list L is updated.

- The process is repeated for the next top object in the list L, until all top-k dominating objects are reported.

We illustrate the STD algorithm in our example. The first repeat is depicted in Figure 4.2. The skyline $SKY(P)$ of P is computed, i.e., $SKY(P) = \{p_{11}, p_{14}, p_{15}\}$. The domination scores of all points in S are computed and inserted in L : $L = \{< p_{14}, 12 >, < p_{11}, 10 >, < p_{15}, 2 >\}$. Then, the exclusive domination region R of p_{14} is selected, p_{14} is reported as top-1, and then is removed from L. The constrained skyline in R contains only p_{13}, and the domination score of p_{13} is computed: $dom(p_{13}) = 10$. The sorted list is updated: $L = \{< p_{11}, 10 >, < p_{13}, 10 > , < p_{15}, 2 >\}$.

The second repeat is depicted in Figure 4.3. The points p_{11}, p_{13} are reported as top-2 and top-3, as they have equal domination scores, whereas all other points in the constrained skylines of their exclusive domination regions have less scores. More specifically, the exclusive domination region R_1 of p_{11} contains only p_6, and the exclusive domination region R_2 of p_{13} is empty. The domination score of p_6 is computed: $dom(p_6) = 5$, and the sorted list is updated:

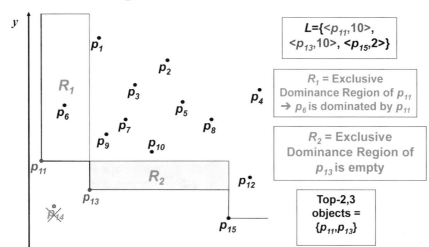

Figure 4.3: Second iteration of STD algorithm.

$L = \{< p_6, 5 >, < p_{15}, 2 >\}$. The top-3 objects have been reported and all objects in L have less domination scores. Therefore the algorithm stops.

The STD algorithm can be viewed as skyline "peeling," since it computes local skylines among objects that have the highest domination score. Moreover, due to its generality it can be applied in any dataset, whereas the computation of the skylines inside STD can be performed by any known off-the-shelf skyline algorithm (i.e., not only the BBS by Papadias et al. (2005a)).

4.3   METHODS BASED ON R-TREE VARIANTS

In multi-dimensional data the STD algorithm can be applied easily, even if the data are indexed in secondary memory. In Papadias et al. (2005a), an R-based mplementation is presented and extensive experiments were conducted.

However, the skyline-based approach may perform many unnecessary score counting, since the partial skylines could have much larger number of objects than k (especially if data have many dimensions).

In Yiu and Mamoulis (2007) and Yiu and Mamoulis (2009), another approach for a top-k dominating query processing is presented. The idea is to process a top-k dominating query as an it aggregate query, when the data are indexed by using hierarchical index structures (such as R-trees by Guttman (1984) and their variants). The computation of the domination score $dop(p)$ of a multi-dimensional object $p \in D$ is in fact an aggregation in D through the R-tree nodes and entries. Therefore, the authors replace the R-tree by an aggregate R-tree (aR-tree by Lazaridis and Mehrotra (2001) and Papadias et al. (2001)), and present their methods for the top-k dominating query processing.

The aR-tree augments to each non-leaf entry of the R-tree an aggregate measure of all data objects in the sub-tree pointed by it. It has been used to speed up the evaluation of spatial aggregate queries, where measures in a spatial region are aggregated. As the domination score of an object p is computed by the number of objects that p dominates, a simple *count* aggregation measure is required for equipping the aR-tree. Therefore, each non-leaf entry stores the count of data objects in its sub-tree.

Five specialized aR-tree-based algorithms have been proposed in Yiu and Mamoulis (2007, 2009):

- Simple Counting Guided (SCG)

- Lightweight Counting Guided (LCG)

- Priority-Based Traversal Algorithm (PBT)

- Upper-bound Based Traversal (UBT), and

- Cost-Based Traversal (CBT)

These algorithms have been compared also with STD, which was implemented with a spatial aggregation technique (for fairness in comparison), and with an optimized version of STD named Iterative Top-k Dominating Algorithm (ITD).

The main strategy of the proposed algorithms is that they use specific score bounding functions applied on the nodes of the aR-tree. For an aR-tree entry e (i.e., a minimum bounding box) whose projection on the ith dimension is the interval $[e[i]^-, e[i]^+]$, its lower corner is denoted by $e^- = (e[1]^-, e[2]^-, \ldots, e[d]^-)$ and its upper corner is denoted by $e^+ = (e[1]^+, e[2]^+, \ldots, e[d]^+)$, where d is the number of dimensions in the dataset D. Both e^- and e^+ do not correspond to actual data objects but they allow us to express domination relationships among objects and minimum bounding boxes conveniently.

Figure 4.4 depicts some examples for the cases of domination. The object p_1 dominates the region of entry e_1, thus it dominates all data objects that are indexed under e_1 (we have a full domination). The same occurs for the regions of entries e_2, e_3, e_4. The object p_2 dominates e_1^+ but not e_1^-, thus it dominates some but not all data objects that are indexed under e_1 (we have a partial domination). Partial domination occurs also for p_3 with entry e_3. Finally, the entire domination region of object p_3 is disjoint with the region of entry e_1, thus it cannot dominate any object indexed under e_1 (we have no domination).

For any aR-tree entry e, the values $dom(e^+)$ and $dom(e^-)$ correspond to the tight-most lower and upper score bounds, respectively, for any object indexed under e.

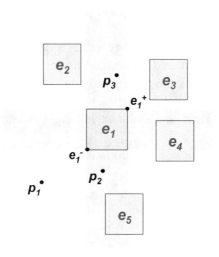

- p_1 dominates the region of e_1, thus it dominates all objects indexed under e_1 (full domination).

- p_2 dominates e_1^+ but not e_1^-, thus it dominates some but not all objects (partial domination).

- p_3 has its entire domination region disjoint with the region of e_1, thus it cannot dominate any object indexed under e_1 (no domination).

Figure 4.4: Domination relationship among aR-tree entries.

4.3.1   ITERATIVE TOP-*K* DOMINATING ALGORITHM (ITD)

The Iterative Top-*k* Dominating Algorithm (ITD by Yiu and Mamoulis (2007) and Yiu and Mamoulis (2009)) is an optimized version of STD, applied with two optimizations that greatly reduce the I/O cost when the data are indexed with an aR-tree.

The first optimization is called *Batch Count*. Instead of iteratively applying separate range queries to compute the scores of the skyline objects, ITD executes them in a recursive batch counting procedure (Batch Count) on the aR-Tree. This procedure is also used as a core counting procedure in the Counting Guided proposed algorithms.

More specifically, when a Batch Count must be conducted for a node z of the aR-tree, then:

- For all entries e of node z, we check:

    – If z is a non-leaf node, and exists an object p of the current candidates that dominates e^+ but not e^-, then the Batch-Count procedure is called recursively for the child node of z.

    – Else z is a leaf node, then all domination scores of the objects p in the current candidate set that dominate e^-, are updated by the count of entry e, i.e., $dom(p) = dom(p) + count(e)$.

This procedure calculates only the non-calculated domination values of the skyline objects and only in the exclusive domination regions, recursively, avoiding recalculations.

The second optimization is that the set structure which keeps all current candidate objects is sorted by a space-filling curve (Hilbert ordering) before applying the Batch Count to increase the compactness of the MBR of a batch. These two optimizations are greatly reducing the I/O cost of STD. The example of Figures 4.2–4.3 illustrate also the processing of ITD algorithm.

However, the skyline-based solutions become inefficient for datasets with large skylines. Moreover, as the data dimensionality increases, the skyline set may become as large as P. An important study in Tiakas et al. (2013) reports that there is a specific dimension (not large), called the *eliminating dimension*, where all domination values in P become zero, thus the skyline of P contains all objects of P ($SKY(P) = P$). Motivated by these observations, the following algorithms proposed by Yiu and Mamoulis (2007) and Yiu and Mamoulis (2009) solve the problem directly, without depending on skyline computations.

4.3.2   SIMPLE COUNTING GUIDED ALGORITHM (SCG)

A main property that holds inside aR-tree is that the domination score of any object p indexed under an entry e is upper bounded by $dom(e^-)$. By using this property, the main idea of SCG (as in Yiu and Mamoulis (2007) and Yiu and Mamoulis (2009)) is to traverse the aR-tree nodes in a descending order of their upper-bound scores.

The rationale is that objects with high domination scores can be retrieved early and, thus, accesses to aR-tree nodes that do not contribute to the result can be avoided. To organize the entries to be visited in descending order of their domination scores, a max-heap structure H is used. The top-k dominating objects are managed by a min-heap structure W as the algorithm progresses, while g is the current kth score in W used for pruning (any object p with a domination score $dom(p) < g$ must not be appeared in the query results).

More specifically, the algorithm takes the following steps.

- The upper bound scores $dom(e^-)$ of the aR-tree root entries are computed in batch (using the Batch-Count procedure of ITD), and are inserted into the max-heap H.

- While the score $dom(e^-)$ of H's top entry e is higher than g, the top entry is deheaped, and the node z pointed by e is visited.

- If z is a non-leaf node, its entries are enheaped, after Batch-Count is called to compute their upper score bounds.

- If z is a leaf node, the exact domination scores of the objects in it are computed in batch and the top-k set W is updated, if applicable.

Figures 4.5–4.6 illustrate the processing of SCG, in our small dataset example, for a top-1 dominating query (for simplicity we selected $k = 1$).

In the aR-tree there are five leaf nodes and their corresponding entries in the root node are e_1, e_2, e_3, e_4, e_5. First, the upper bound scores for the root entries are computed with the batch-counting procedure, i.e., $dom(e_1^-) = 14$, $dom(e_2^-) = 9$, $dom(e_3^-) = 7$, $dom(e_4^-) = 3$, $dom(e_5^-) =$

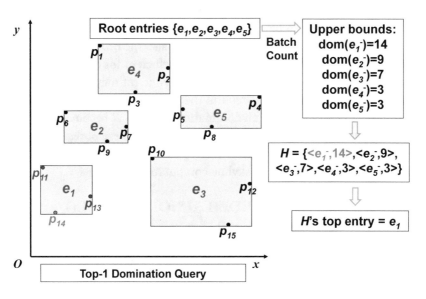

Figure 4.5: SCG algorithm—constructing the heap H.

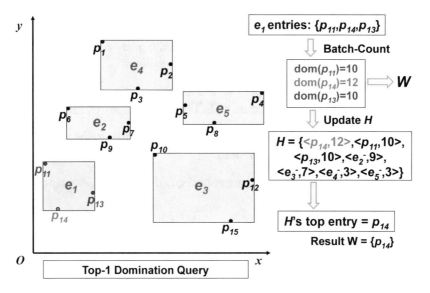

Figure 4.6: SCG algorithm—computing necessary scores.

3. The scores are then inserted into the max-heap: $H = \{< e_1^-, 14 >, < e_2^-, 9 >, < e_3^-, 7 >, < e_4^-, 3 >, < e_5^-, 3 >\}$.

Since e_1 has the highest upper bound score it will be accessed next. As it is a leaf node, the exact domination scores of all entries in e_1 are computed in batch, i.e., $dom(p_{11}) = 10$, $dom(p_{14}) = 12$, $dom(p_{13}) = 10$. The heap H is updated: $H = \{< p_{14}, 12 >, < p_{11}, 10 >, < p_{13}, 10 >, < e_2^-, 9 >, < e_3^-, 7 >, < e_4^-, 3 >, < e_5^-, 3 >\}$.

Since p_{14} has the highest exact domination score of all the remaining entries, it is guaranteed to be the top-1 result.

4.3.3   LIGHTWEIGHT COUNTING GUIDED ALGORITHM (LCG)

The Lightweight Counting Guided Algorithm (LCG as in Yiu and Mamoulis (2007) and Yiu and Mamoulis (2009)) is an optimized version of SCG. The main idea of the algorithm is to replace the tight upper score bound $dom(e^-)$ by a looser and cheaper to compute bound $dom^u(e)$.

The algorithm processes exactly as SCG with the difference that the Batch-Count procedure is replaced by a Light-Batch-Count procedure, which is a variation of Batch-Count. More specifically, when bounds for a set of non-leaf entries are counted, the algorithm avoids expensive accesses at aR-tree leaf nodes, by using entries at non-leaf nodes to derive looser bounds.

In our small dataset example, Figures 4.5–4.6 illustrate also the processing of LCG, with the difference that the following looser bounds are used: $dom^u(e_1) = 15$, $dom^u(e_2) = 9$, $dom^u(e_3) = 9$, $dom^u(e_4) = 3$, $dom^u(e_5) = 3$. The bounds are calculated without processing the p_i objects but by using only the aggregation counts of nodes e_i.

For example, the $dom^u(e_1)$ value is equal to 15 because e_1 fully or partially dominates all other e_i regions, i.e., $dom^u(e_1) = count(e_1) + count(e_2) + count(e_3) + count(e_4) + count(e_5) = 3 + 3 + 3 + 3 + 3 = 15$. The $dom^u(e_3)$ value is equal to 9 because e_3 fully or partially dominates only the regions e_4, e_5 regions, i.e., $dom^u(e_3) = count(e_3) + count(e_4) + count(e_5) = 3 + 3 + 3 = 9$.

Since again e_1 has the highest bound score dom^u, it will be accessed first, and the processing in our example continuous as previously.

4.3.4   PRIORITY- AND UPPER BOUND-BASED TRAVERSAL ALGORITHMS (PBT, UBT)

The Counting-Guided approaches, may access some aR-tree nodes more than once due to the application of counting operations for the visited entries. In Yiu and Mamoulis (2007) and Yiu and Mamoulis (2009), Priority-Based Traversal (PBT) Algorithms are also proposed, where the general idea is that instead of computing upper bounds of visited entries by explicit counting to defer score computations for entries, and maintain lower and upper bounds for them during the tree is traversed. Score bounds for visited entries are gradually refined when more nodes are accessed, until the result is finalized with the help of them. For this method to be effective, the tree is traversed with a carefully designed priority order aiming at minimizing I/O cost.

The general PBT, during traversal, maintains a set S of visited aR-tree entries, and loose upper $dom^u(e)$ and lower $dom^l(e)$ score bounds for the entries e that have been seen so far. The top-k dominating objects are managed by a min-heap structure W as the algorithm progresses, while g is the current kth score in W used for pruning. More specifically, the algorithm works as follows.

- First, the root node is loaded, and its entries are inserted into S after upper score bounds have been derived from information in the root node.

- While S contains non-leaf entries, the non-leaf entry e_z with the highest priority is removed from S, the corresponding tree node z is visited, and: (i) the dom^u, dom^l scores of existing entries in S that partially dominating e_z are refined using the contents of z, (ii) the dom^u, dom^l values for the contents of z are computed and inserted into S.

- W is updated with objects/entries of higher dom^l than g.

- Finally, entries are pruned from S if: (i) they cannot lead to objects that may be included in W and (ii) they are not partially dominated by entries leading to objects that can reach W.

The Upper-bound Based Traversal (UBT) Algorithm is the PBT algorithm with a priority traversal order guided by the highest upper bound score (dom^u) entries e_z. Such an order would visit the objects that have high probability to be in the top-k dominating results early.

The execution of UBT in our small dataset example is similar as in Figures 4.5–4.6, but instead of the heap H the set S is used. We denote the score bounds of an entry e in S by the interval $dom(e) = [dom^l(e), dom^u(e)]$. UBT accesses the root node and its entries are inserted into S after their lower/upper bound scores are derived: $dom(e_1) = [0, 15]$, $dom(e_2) = [0, 9]$, $dom(e_3) = [0, 9]$, $dom(e_4) = [0, 3]$, $dom(e_5) = [0, 3]$. The entry e_1 again has the highest dom^u score in S, thus is removed and its containing objects are accessed. The score bounds for p_{11}, p_{14}, and p_{13} are computed and p_{14} is again reported as the top-1 result.

4.3.5   COST-BASED TRAVERSAL ALGORITHM (CBT)

A closer look into UBT reveals that the upper score bounds alone may not offer the best priority order for traversing the tree. S can grow very large if there are many partial domination relationships between its entries. To minimize the partially dominating entry pairs in S, the visited nodes are prioritized based on their level at the tree. In addition, between entries at the highest level in S, the one with the highest upper bound is chosen to find the objects with high scores early. This variation of UBT is the Cost-Based Traversal (CBT) Algorithm.

4.4   INDEX-FREE ALGORITHMS

In Yiu and Mamoulis (2009) there is also a study for the evaluation of top-k dominating queries on non-indexed data, assuming that data objects are stored in random order in a disk file.

A practically viable solution is to first bulk-load an aR-tree from the dataset and then compute top-k dominating objects using the previous proposed algorithms. The bulk-loading step requires externally sorting the objects, which is known to scale well for large datasets. However, external sorting may incur multiple I/O passes over data.

In Yiu and Mamoulis (2009), two specialized algorithms, Coarse-grained Filter Algorithm (CRS) and Fine-grained Filter Algorithm (FN), are proposed to determine the top-k dominating objects with only a constant number of data passes, by using a filter-refinement framework. These algorithms require three passes over data.

- The first pass is the counting pass, which employs a memory grid structure to keep track of object count in cells, while scanning over the data. This structure is then used to derive lower/upper bound scores of objects in the next pass.

- The second pass is the filter pass, which applies pruning rules to discard unqualified objects and keep the remaining ones in a candidate set.

- The refinement pass, being the final pass, performs a scan over the data to count the exact domination scores of all candidate objects. Eventually, the top-k dominating objects are returned.

Both algorithms use the previously defined bounds in Section 4.3 and their only difference is that FN tightens more the bounds of candidate points than CRS, by using the dom^u scores.

4.5 SUBSPACE PROGRESSIVE ALGORITHMS

R-trees and their variants have been extensively used in the literature to support a broad range of queries over multi-dimensional data sets, including the top-k dominating queries (see Yiu and Mamoulis (2007), Yiu and Mamoulis (2009), Papadias et al. (2005a), and Papadias et al. (2001)). Their major limitation is that since all dimensions are used to organize the dataset, subspace search requires a series of projection operations which affects efficiency due to increased I/O activity. Moreover, the resulting indexing scheme becomes inefficient even for processing queries involving the whole set of dimensions, due to the dimensionality curse. Summarizing the main limitations on the previous approaches, we have that:

- they lack progressiveness (they report the k best objects at the end of the processing;

- they require a multi-dimensional index or they build a grid-based index on-the-fly, which suffers from performance degradation, especially in high dimensionalities; and

- they do not support vertically decomposed data, and efficient query processing in subsets of dimensions (subspace queries).

Alternative approaches have been proposed organizing each dimension separately, resulting in a column-oriented (i.e., vertically decomposed) physical data organization. Column-oriented storage shows significant performance improvements in specific types of operations and, moreover, offers a completely independent treatment of dimensions, thus supporting flexible query processing involving a subset of dimensions. This way, the rest of the dimensions do not participate in query processing, and thus, query evaluation becomes more efficient. A column-oriented organization is a natural and intuitive choice taking into account that it is impossible to provide a full-dimensional indexing scheme for every $2^d - 1$ possible subsets of dimensions.

Motivated by these observations, four algorithms are proposed in Tiakas et al. (2011): *Basic Scan Algorithm* (BSA), *Union Algorithm* (UA), *Reverse Algorithm* (RA), and *Differential Algorithm* (DA), which:

- they support efficient subspace queries for every possible subsets of dimensions ($2^d - 1$); and

- they provide the top-*k* results progressively, i.e., they return to the user the best item first, then the second best and so on. This also enables early termination if adequate results have been returned.

The architecture of the physical organization of the proposed methods in Tiakas et al. (2011) is depicted in Figure 4.7. Each dimension is organized separately by a B^+-tree, which facilitates random as well as sorted access (any other index which facilitates random and sorted access can also be used). Each B^+-tree indexes the attribute values of the specific dimension. A user may select any subset of dimensions, whereas query execution is supported by the use of a Least Recently Used (LRU) buffer.

An additional B^+-tree is used (called Set-B^+) for intermediate computations which are kept on disk (no need of additional main memory storage). Sorted access is not required in Set-B^+ thus a hash index can also be used.

Set-B^+ is used by the top-*k* query algorithm for intermediate computations. At the beginning of any top-*k* query, the Set-B^+ is empty. During execution, the IDs of scanned objects are inserted into the Set-B^+ and several counters are updated. By using this approach, all intermediate results are kept on disk (if needed) and there is no need of additional main memory storage. The Set-B^+ shares the same LRU buffer with all other data B^+-trees.

The proposed algorithms in Tiakas et al. (2011) are using the concept of terminating objects. A *terminating object* is an object whose attribute values on all dimensions of interest have been retrieved (scanned) via sorted access on their indexes.

The main idea of the proposed algorithms is to scan on B^+-trees of the selected dimensions from the beginning in a round-robin manner to discover the terminating objects one by one, to estimate and calculate (if necessary) their domination scores that are maintained in a max-heap, and to extract them progressively one by one from the max-heap when their scores are definitely greater than the rest objects. The main difference between the proposed algorithms is the way that they compute the exact domination scores of the detected terminating objects.

An example of detection of terminating objects is depicted in Figure 4.8, after the organization of the dataset of our main example. Two B^+-trees are used, one for the *x* dimension

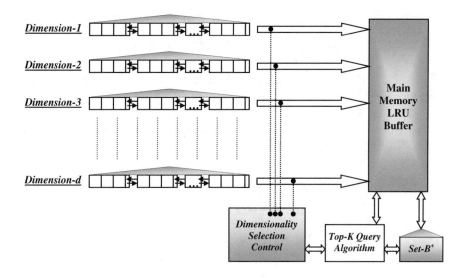

Figure 4.7: Data organization utilized by BSA, UA, RA, and DA.

and one for the y dimension. The objects are sorted by their values in each B^+-tree. During the round-robin scan, the first detected terminating object is p_{14}, requiring four value accesses. The second detected terminating object is p_{13} and requires another three value accesses. The third detected terminating object is p_{11} and requires another three value accesses. This process is continuous until all required objects are retrieved through the proposed algorithms.

Due to the sorted order of values in the B^+-trees, all objects with the same value in a specific dimension appear sequentially in the leaf level. This group of objects is called an *equality group* (the equality group of an object p is denoted as E_p). In the example of Figure 4.8, the objects p_7, p_8 have the same y value (65), thus they lie in the same equality group ($E_{p_7} = E_{p_8} = \{p_7, p_8\}$).

The sorted order position of a terminating object p is its position in the dimension that was detected and is denoted as $pos(p)$. In the example of Figure 4.8 we have $pos(p_{14}) = 2$, $pos(p_{13}) = 4$, $pos(p_{11}) = 5$.

The sorted order position of an object p in a dimension i is denoted as $Lpos_i(p)$. In the example of Figure 4.8 we have $Lpos_x(p_{11}) = 1$, $Lpos_y(p_{13}) = 3$. In case the object lies in an equality group the left-most position of the group is considered. In the example of Figure 4.8 we have $Lpos_y(p_8) = 8$ and $Lpos_y(p_7) = 8$.

The proposed algorithms are based on the following fundamental properties.

- If in a dimension an object p has been detected with an equality group E_p, then p may be dominated only by objects that are before E_p in the sorted order of that dimension,

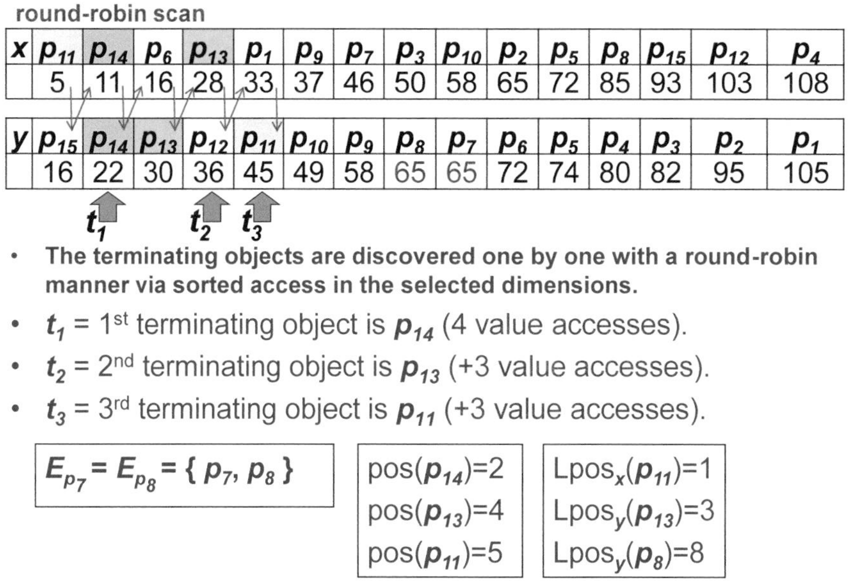

round-robin scan

x	p_{11}	p_{14}	p_6	p_{13}	p_1	p_9	p_7	p_3	p_{10}	p_2	p_5	p_8	p_{15}	p_{12}	p_4
	5	11	16	28	33	37	46	50	58	65	72	85	93	103	108

y	p_{15}	p_{14}	p_{13}	p_{12}	p_{11}	p_{10}	p_9	p_8	p_7	p_6	p_5	p_4	p_3	p_2	p_1
	16	22	30	36	45	49	58	65	65	72	74	80	82	95	105

t_1 t_2 t_3

- The terminating objects are discovered one by one with a round-robin manner via sorted access in the selected dimensions.
- t_1 = 1st terminating object is p_{14} (4 value accesses).
- t_2 = 2nd terminating object is p_{13} (+3 value accesses).
- t_3 = 3rd terminating object is p_{11} (+3 value accesses).

$E_{p_7} = E_{p_8} = \{ p_7, p_8 \}$

$pos(p_{14})=2$	$Lpos_x(p_{11})=1$
$pos(p_{13})=4$	$Lpos_y(p_{13})=3$
$pos(p_{11})=5$	$Lpos_y(p_8)=8$

Figure 4.8: Detection of terminating objects and other definitions.

and it may dominate objects that are after E_p. If there are other objects in E_p, they may dominate p, may be dominated by p, or they may not dominate each other.

- According to the previous property, if in a dimension an object p has been detected as a terminating object, it cannot dominate more than $N - pos(p) + |E_p| - 1$ objects, where $N = |D|$ the total number of the objects in the dataset D (N is the dataset cardinality).

- This allows an immediate estimation of the domination score of any terminating object t at the moment it was detected, $estdom(t) = N - pos(t) + |E_t| - 1$.

The main idea of the proposed algorithms is: to round-robin scan on B$^+$-trees of the selected dimensions discover the terminating objects one by one, estimate and exact calculate (if necessary) their domination scores that are maintained in a max-heap H, and extract them progressively one by one from H when their scores are definitely greater than the rest objects. The main difference between the proposed algorithms is the way that they compute the exact domination scores toward performance improvement.

4.5.1   BASIC SCAN ALGORITHM (BSA)

The Basic Scan Algorithm (BSA) is based on the previous fundamental properties. It keeps all discovered terminating objects in a max-heap H prioritized on their estimated domination scores. During processing, only the exact domination values of the top estimated objects are calculated, updating the heap as necessary. The following important property provides the condition for a terminating object to be reported as the next top result, enabling the progressive behavior of the algorithm.

- If t_1, t_2 are the top-2 terminating objects in the heap H, and $dom(t_1) \geq estdom(t_2)$ (or $dom(t_1) \geq dom(t_2)$ in case t_2 has an exact score), then t_1 can be immediately reported as the next top result.

Assembling all together, after initializing the heap H, the LRU-Buffer and the Set-B$^+$, the main algorithmic procedure of BSA is the following.

- If H is empty then scan and detect the next two terminating objects, else only the next one, give them their estimated scores, and insert them into H.

- Extract the top-1 object t_1 from H and if it has not an exact domination score then calculate it ($dom(t_1)$). Get also the top-2 object t_2 from H (without extraction and calculation).

- If $dom(t_1) \geq estdom(t_2)$ (or $dom(t_1) \geq dom(t_2)$ in case t_2 has an exact score), then report t_1 as the next top dominating result, or else go to the first step.

- The process is repeated until all top-k dominating objects are reported progressively.

The exact domination score of a terminating object t in BSA is computed based on the domination checks between t and all objects that are in the same equality group with t and after t in the dimension that t was detected. Each domination check is performed by retrieving all attribute values of these objects using random accesses.

Let us present an example of BSA execution by applying a top-1 dominating query to the data depicted in Figure 4.9. Initially, the first two terminating objects t_1, t_2 are detected and enheaped, by visiting the objects in the B$^+$-trees for dimensions x and y with the (round-robin) order. More specifically, the scan goes: $p_{11}, p_{15}, p_{14}, p_{14}$. Therefore, p_{14} is the first terminating object (detected after four value accesses) and is enheaped with an estimated domination value of $estdom(p_{14}) = N - pos(p_{14}) + |E_{p_{14}}| - 1 = 15 - 2 + 1 - 1 = 13$. Then, the second terminating object p_{13} (detected after three more value accesses by visiting p_6, p_{13}, p_{13}) is enheaped with an estimated domination value of $estdom(p_{13}) = N - pos(p_{13}) + |E_{p_{13}}| - 1 = 15 - 4 + 1 - 1 = 11$.

In the next step, p_{14} is extracted from the top of the heap H (as it has the maximum score), and its exact domination score is computed by checking whether it dominates the following objects $p_{13}, p_{12}, p_{11}, p_{10}, p_9, p_8, p_7, p_6, p_5, p_4, p_3, p_2, p_1$, requiring another 13 sequential value accesses in the y dimension and 13 random value accesses in the x dimension (to retrieve both coordinates and check domination). As p_{14} does not dominate p_{11}, its final exact domination score is $dom(p_{14}) = 12$. It holds that $dom(p_{14}) = 12 > 11 = estdom(p_{13})$, thus the object p_{14} can be

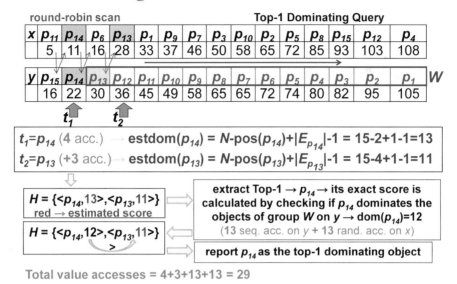

Figure 4.9: BSA algorithm processing.

immediately reported as the top-1 dominating object. BSA requires $4 + 3 + 13 + 13 = 29$ total value accesses.

4.5.2   UNION ALGORITHM (UA)

Although BSA is progressive, it performs a significant number of random accesses for domination checking, and this may lead to a significant I/O cost. The Union Algorithm (UA) alleviates this problem as it does not require any explicit domination checks among data objects. UA is a variation of BSA. The fundamental difference is that UA uses a different mechanism for exact domination value computation. It takes advantage from an important property (union property) that can calculate the domination score of a terminating object t by using the objects that have already been retrieved before t in the selected dimensions, and not after t (that BSA does).

Union Property: If t is a terminating object, and we collect in a set U_t, all objects that lie before the equality groups of t in the selected dimensions, and we collect also in a set UE_t all the equivalent objects to t (i.e., UE_t is the intersection of all the equality groups of t in the selected dimensions), then it holds that: $dom(t) = N - |U_t| - |UE_t| - 1$.

This comes from the fact that t cannot dominate the following: (i) objects that have a better value in at least one dimension (i.e., lie before the equality group of t); (ii) objects that have the same attribute values in all selected dimensions (equivalent objects); and (iii) itself.

Therefore, the exact domination score of a terminating object t in UA is computed based to the union property. The main idea is to compute the sets U_t and UE_t, by scanning the B$^+$-

trees again from the beginning in all selected dimensions, and stop when the equality group of t has been reached. It is important to note that during the round-robin scan for the retrieving of t, all scanning pointers stop at $pos(t)$ (or $pos(t) - 1$), thus to detect the $Lpos$ positions of the equality groups of t and at the same time to compute the sets U_t and UE_t, we scan again from the beginning each dimension separately.

It is also important to note that the required sets U_t, UE_t are not implemented as separate structures and no additional space is required. This is because we are not interested in the specific final objects that are contained, but only in their cardinalities (e.g., $|U_t|$, $|UE_t|$), and this is conducted with specific counters and counting in the Set-B$^+$ structure (as they contain objects that have already been retrieved).

The main algorithmic procedure of UA is the following.

- It progresses as the BSA algorithm.

- When an exact domination score calculation is required, the cardinalities $|U_t|$ and $|UE_t|$ are computed by scanning the B$^+$-trees again from the beginning in all selected dimensions sequentially one by one, and stop when the equality groups of t have been entirely scanned.

- Two specific counters (one for each set) are updated in the Set-B$^+$ structure during the scanning.

In our running example (see Figure 4.10), the only difference is that when p_{14} is extracted from the top of the heap, the calculation phase of the UA algorithm computes the size of its union set $|U_{p_{14}}| = |\{p_{11}, p_{15}\}| = 2$ and of the set of its equivalent objects $|UE_{p_{14}}|=0$, by making four total value accesses from the beginning. Therefore, the domination score of p_{14} is calculated as follows: $dom(p_{14}) = 15 - 2 - 0 - 1 = 12$. Now the algorithm terminates performing in total 4+3+4=11 value accesses (less than BSA and not random).

4.5.3   REVERSE ALGORITHM (RA)

Although UA eliminates the drawbacks of BSA, it has a serious limitation: when the extracted terminating objects have high positions (especially in anti-correlated data), or there are a lot of selected dimensions, the total number of required value accesses in set calculations is significantly increased and this may produce additional I/O cost.

The Reverse Algorithm (RA), takes advantage of the fact that all positions of the detected terminating object t in the selected dimensions are less than or equal to $pos(t)$. Therefore, instead of scanning the B$^+$-trees from the beginning (as UA does), RA scans backward from $pos(t)$ and stops when the equality group of t has been retrieved completely in each selected dimension (i.e., its $Lpos$ positions reached).

Initially, the set U_t contains all objects found so far during the round-robin scan to the position $pos(t)$, and during the reverse scanning, all detected objects are definitely lying after

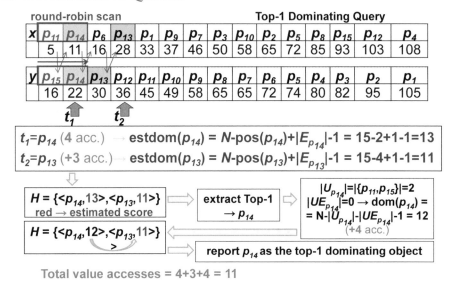

Figure 4.10: UA algorithm processing.

(or inside) the equality groups of t, thus they removed from U_t. Therefore, when the reverse scanning is completed U_t will have the appropriate number of objects. It is important to note again that we are not interested in the specific final objects that are contained in $|U_t|$, $|UE_t|$, but only in their size (e.g., $|U_t|$, $|UE_t|$), and this is conducted with specific counters and counting in the Set-B$^+$.

Assembling altogether, the main algorithmic procedure of RA is the following.

- It progresses as the UA algorithm.

- It takes advantage of the fact that all positions of the detected terminating object t in the selected dimensions are less than or equal to $pos(t)$.

- It scans backward from $pos(t)$ and stops when the equality group of t has been retrieved completely in each selected dimension.

- The specific counters for the cardinalities $|U_t|$ and $|UE_t|$ are updated in an opposite way in the Set-B$^+$ structure during the scanning.

In our running example (see Figure 4.11), the only difference is that when p_{14} is extracted from the top of the heap H, the calculation phase of the RA algorithm computes the size of its union set $|U_{p14}| = 4 - 2 = 2$ (by subtracting the 2 different objects p_6 and p_{14} that are found during the reverse scan from the positions of the last detected terminating object p_{13} after the initial round-robin scan), and of the set of its equivalent objects $|UE_{p14}| = 0$, by making only

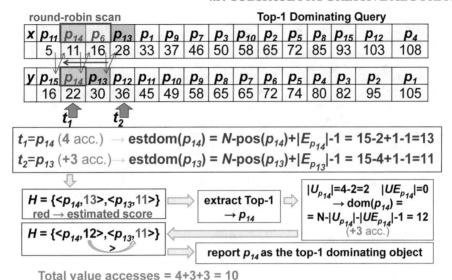

Figure 4.11: RA algorithm processing.

3 value accesses. Therefore, the domination score of p_{14} is calculated as follows: $dom(p_{14}) = 15 - 2 - 0 - 1 = 12$. Now the algorithm terminates performing in total $4 + 3 + 3 = 10$ value accesses.

4.5.4   DIFFERENTIAL ALGORITHM (DA)

The Differential Algorithm (DA) is based on the idea that when there is a need to compute the exact domination score of a terminating object t, we can select a previously determined convenient terminating object t_p (best object under specific criteria) whose exact domination score has been already computed. Forward and backward scans (combining the advantages of UA,RA) are performed taking into consideration the $Lpos$ positions of t and t_p:

- if $Lpos(t_p) < Lpos(t)$ scans forward from t_p to t (increase counters for $|U_t|$ and $|UE_t|$) and

- if $Lpos(t_p) > Lpos(t)$ scans backward from t_p to t (decrease counters for $|U_t|$ and $|UE_t|$).

Therefore, if object t is positioned after t_p in a selected dimension, then the algorithm scans forward from t_p to t in the B$^+$-tree of this dimension and increases specific counters into the Set-B$^+$ structure for the visited objects, otherwise it scans backward and decreases specific counters into the Set-B$^+$ structure for the visited objects. Finally, the exact domination value of the terminating object t is computed using the updated visits set counters and the same formula

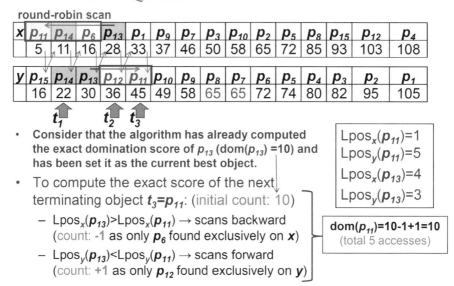

Figure 4.12: Differential calculation with DA.

as in UA. The positions of t and t_p that are checked are their *Lpos* positions which are also stored in the Set-B$^+$ structure during processing.

For example, let us consider that the algorithm has already computed the exact domination score of p_{13} ($dom(p_{13}) = 10$) and has been set it as the current best object (see Figure 4.12). To compute the exact score of terminating object p_{11}, we initially set $dom(p_{11}) = dom(p_{13}) = 10$ and we scan backward in dimension x (as $Lpos_x(p_{11}) < Lpos_x(p_{13})$) till p_{11} is found. During the scan only one object (p_6) was found exclusively on x dimension, thus we subtract 1 from the score (current $dom(p_{11}) = 9$). Now we scan forward in dimension y (as $Lpos_y(p_{11}) > Lpos_y(p_{13})$) until p_{11} is found. During scan only one object (p_{12}) was newly found on y dimension, thus we add 1 to the score ($dom(p_{11}) = 10$). Thus, the final exact domination score of p_{11} is $dom(p_{11}) = 10$, and the calculation procedure required a total of 5 value accesses.

A good criterion for the selection of the best terminating object t_p during processing is to take into account the minimum absolute difference of positions. Therefore, when a newly discovered terminating object t minimizes the absolute difference of *Lpos* positions with the current best object t_p, then it becomes the new best object. Using this technique the total number of value accesses is further decreasing.

Moreover, to even further decrease the number of value accesses and the corresponding I/O operations, a collection of pruning rules has been designed toward performance boost, which can be applied in all proposed algorithms (BSA, UA, RA, DA). Three types of pruning rules are proposed in Tiakas et al. (2011), according to their applicability to the algorithm parts:

- *Discard Rules* (DRs), which update all objects that can be discarded during the scanning for the next candidate terminating object;

- *Early Pruning Rules* (EPRs), which are applied before the computation of the exact domination value of the selected terminating object; and

- *Internal Pruning Rules* (IPRs), which are applied during exact score computation.

For further details, see Tiakas et al. (2011).

4.6   METRIC-BASED APPROACHES

All previous algorithms address the problem in settings where data objects are multi-dimensional objects with static attributes, and multi-dimensional indexing is issued for efficient processing. However, there are domains where we only have access to the distance between two objects. In cases like these, attributes reflect distances from a set of input objects and are dynamically generated as the input objects change. For example, attributes may correspond to distances from specific query points. Consequently, the previous algorithms cannot be applied, despite the fact that the domination relation is still meaningful and valid.

In Tiakas et al. (2014) and Tiakas et al. (2016) there is an extended study for processing top-k dominating queries over distance-based dynamic attribute vectors, defined over a metric space. Four progressive algorithms are proposed: Skyline-Based Algorithm (SBA), Aggregation-Based Algorithm (ABA), Pruning-Based Algorithms (PBA1) and (PBA2), from which PBA2 shows the best overall performance.

The proposed algorithms can be applied on a dataset D in which a distance function $d()$ has been defined which quantifies the dissimilarity between data objects in D, i.e., D equipped with d is a metric space. The user provides a set of query objects $Q = \{q_1, q_2, \ldots, q_m\}$. Then, for any two objects $p, r \in D$, p dominates r, if and only if p has an equal or smaller distance than r to all query objects $q_i \in Q$, and p has a smaller distance than r to at least one query object. In case the objects p and r have exactly the same distance from q_i, i.e., $d(p, q_i) = d(r, q_i)$, $\forall i = 1, \ldots, m$, they are called equivalent.

The set of objects in D which are not dominated by any other object (according to the distances from Q) is called the metric space skyline with respect to Q, denoted as $MSS(Q)$. A metric-based top-k dominating query returns the k objects with the maximum domination scores *dom* in D respecting the previous defined domination relationship, and is denoted as $MSD(Q, k)$.

Figure 4.13 shows a top-3 dominating query in a metric space with 25 two-dimensional objects, under the Euclidean distance. Two query objects q_1 and q_2 are also depicted. Object p_1 is definitely the top-1 object, as it is the nearest neighbor of both query objects q_1, q_2. Since no other object lies inside either circle $C_1(q_1, d(q_1, p_1))$ or circle $C_2(q_2, d(q_2, p_1))$, p_1 dominates all other objects and its domination score is $dom(p_1) = 24$. The second nearest neighbor of q_1 is

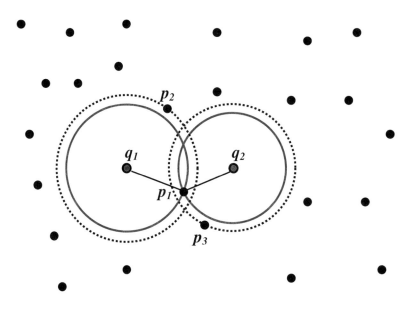

Figure 4.13: Metric-based top-3 dominating query.

p_2, whereas that of q_2 is p_3. Since $d(p_2, q_1) < d(p_3, q_1)$ (p_3 lies outside circle $C_3(q_1, d(p_2, q_1))$) and $d(p_2, q_2) > d(p_3, q_2)$ (p_2 lies outside circle $C_4(q_2, d(p_3, q_2))$), p_2 and p_3 do not dominate each other. However, p_2 and p_3 dominate all other objects since there are no objects lying inside the corresponding dotted circles (except p_1). Thus, their domination score is $dom(p_2) = 22$ and $dom(p_3) = 22$, whereas remaining objects have a domination score less than 22. Therefore, the set $\{p_1, p_2, p_3\}$ is the final answer to the top-3 dominating query based on query objects q_1 and q_2.

The data organization used by the proposed algorithms in Tiakas et al. (2014) and Tiakas et al. (2016) is depicted in Figure 4.14. Among the available metric-based indexes the M-tree by Ciaccia et al. (1997) has been selected which is well appreciated due to its simplicity, its resemblance to the B-tree, its excellent performance and its ability to handle dynamic datasets (i.e., insertions and deletions). However, the proposed methods are orthogonal to the indexing scheme used, as long as incremental k-nearest-neighbor retrieval is supported. In addition to the M-tree, an auxiliary B$^+$-tree (denoted as AuxB$^+$-tree) is being used, which serves as a temporary index for intermediate computations which are kept on disk (no need of additional main memory storage, similarly with the Set-B$^+$ that used in BSA, UA, RA, and DA approaches). Initially, the AuxB$^+$-tree is empty. Sorted access in AuxB$^+$-tree is not required thus a hash index can also

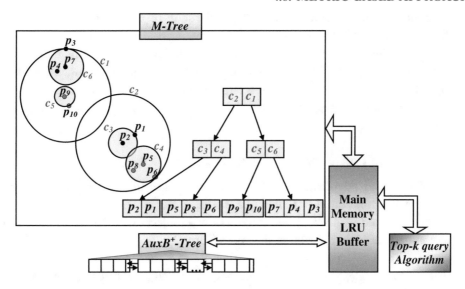

Figure 4.14: Data organization used by metric-based top-k dominating algorithms.

be used. Both the M-tree and the AuxB^+-tree are supported by an LRU buffer which reduces the overall I/O cost.

The proposed algorithms Skyline-Based Algorithm (SBA), Aggregation-Based Algorithm (ABA), and Pruning-Based Algorithms (PBA1, PBA2) have the following properties: (i) they support efficient query processing in dynamic environments; (ii) they provide the top-k results progressively; and (iii) PBA1, PBA2 use special pruning mechanisms in the metric-space to further increase the performance.

4.6.1 SKYLINE-BASED ALGORITHM (SBA)

The Skyline-Based Algorithm (SBA) is based directly on the observation of Papadias et al. (2005a) that the top-1 dominating object belongs to the skyline. The process of SBA is the following.

- The metric skyline S of D with respect to Q is computed ($MSS(Q)$).

- The top-1 dominating object p in D from S is computed, by computing the domination scores of all objects in S.

- p is reported and removed from the dataset D.

- The process is repeated until all top-k objects have been reported (then they are re-inserted in D).

For the metric-space skyline query $MSS(Q)$, the state-of-the-art algorithm B^2MS^2 proposed in Fuhry et al. (2009) is used, implemented to manage M-tree nodes.

SBA reports the top-k results in a progressive manner. However, this method has two important limitations: (i) it performs many unnecessary score computations, since the skyline is often larger than k and (ii) when there is a large number of query objects, the skyline grows significantly and in some cases approaches the data set cardinality. These characteristics may lead to significant performance degradation.

4.6.2 AGGREGATION-BASED ALGORITHM (ABA)

The Aggregation-Based Algorithm (ABA) takes advantages of the properties of the sum-aggregate nearest-neighbor queries studied in Papadias et al. (2005b). A sum-aggregate nearest neighbor query, denoted as $ANN(Q, k)$, contains the k objects with the minimum aggregate distance (computed based on the sum of distances from Q).

Property-1: If an object p dominates another object r then p will be returned before r in the result list of a top-h aggregate nearest neighbor query $ANN(Q, h)$ by using the sum-aggregate function (sum of distances from Q).

But there is a problem with that property: the value of h is not known to retrieve the top-k dominating objects with a single ANN query, through filtering and refinement approach (we can take $h \geq k$ but we do not know how big would be enough). However, another important property can be used:

Property-2: The first sum-aggregate nearest-neighbor of Q is always a metric space skyline object, i.e., $ANN(Q, 1) \in MSS(Q)$.

Therefore, the skyline computation that SBA does is not required and this enables an alternative methodology which is the main process of the ABA algorithm.

- Initially, the top-1 sum-aggregate nearest-neighbor object p of Q is computed, i.e., $p = ANN(Q, 1)$. Since p is a skyline object, there is no object that dominates p. Therefore, there are no objects inside p's dominator region and additionally p dominates all other objects lying into its domination region. This ensures that the top-1 dominating object cannot lie into the dominator/domination regions of p.

- Thus, the top-1 dominating object is searched in the rest of the dataset (remaining region C). Candidates are collected in set C by performing simple range queries centered at the query objects $q_1, q_2, \ldots, q_m$ with radius $d(p, q_1), d(p, q_2), \ldots, d(p, q_m)$, respectively.

- The dominating scores of all objects in C are computed and the top-1 dominating object t is retrieved.

- Object t is reported and removed from the dataset D.

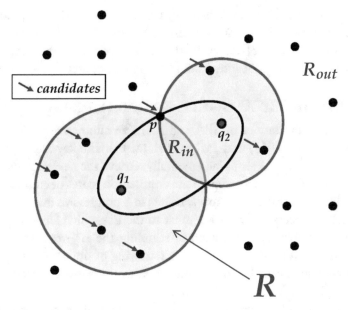

Figure 4.15: ABA algorithm processing.

- The process is repeated until all top-k objects have been reported (then they are re-inserted in D).

For the aggregate nearest neighbor query $ANN(Q, 1)$ the MBM algorithm of Papadias et al. (2005b) is used, which is the state-of-the-art algorithm for ANN queries with the sum-aggregate function. The main difference is that the MBM method is implemented to manage M-tree nodes instead of R-tree nodes supported by the original proposal. The range queries are efficiently supported by the M-tree structure. The candidate objects of the set C and their domination scores are kept and updated into the AuxB$^+$-tree.

For a better view of those candidates let us consider the example of Figure 4.15 for a top-1 dominating query with two query objects q_1, q_2. After $p = ANN(Q, 1)$ is retrieved, the candidates are the objects contained inside the circles with centers the query objects and radii their corresponding distances from p (shaded area R). In our case, there are no objects inside the circle intersection area R_{in} (dominator region of p), as p cannot be dominated. Moreover, there are no objects inside the elliptic area, since p is the first sum-aggregate nearest-neighbor of Q. Additionally, p dominates all objects outside the two circles R_{out} (domination region of p).

ABA reports the top-k results in a progressive manner. It benefits from the fact that in most cases it is expected that the cost of the ANN query plus the cost of the simple range queries, is lower than the cost of a complete skyline computation (as performed by SBA). However, the limitations of ABA are as follows: (i) it recalculates up to k times the domination scores of some nearest neighbor candidate objects of C; and (ii) when the cardinality of Q increases we must perform a large number of range queries, which deteriorates the performance of the algorithm, and when the query objects are far from each other, the range queries may return a large number of candidates, thus C grows significantly leading to high computational costs.

4.6.3 PRUNING-BASED ALGORITHMS (PBA1, PBA2)

Based on the significant limitations of SBA and ABA, an alternative pruning-based approach is proposed in Tiakas et al. (2014) and Tiakas et al. (2016). The key idea behind the Pruning-Based Algorithms (PBA1, PBA2) is to incrementally retrieve the nearest neighbors of the query objects in a round-robin fashion, to compute the domination scores of common neighbors, and, under certain conditions, to extract the top-k results in a progressive manner.

The algorithmic process of PBA1 is similar to the RA which already described in a previous section. The difference is that instead of scanning the B$^+$-trees values (since we don't have multiple B$^+$-trees but a single M-tree), the retrieving of the nearest neighbors from each query object is done dynamically by an incremental nearest neighbor retrieval process which is efficiently supported by the M-tree implementation of Ciaccia et al. (1997).

Now the notion of a terminating object in the metric space is equivalent to the notion of a *common neighbor object*, which is an object that has been discovered in the nearest neighbor order lists of all query objects during the incremental NN retrieval (not necessarily with the same position order).

Again we have an upper bound for the domination score of a retrieved object o_i, which is used as an estimation of its score denoted as *estdom*(o_i). This bound is based on the property: if an object o_i has been retrieved as the $(r_{i,j})$th nearest-neighbor of query object q_j (where $r_{i,j}$ is the rank position of o_i in the nearest neighbor order list of q_j), then: $dom(o_i) \leq N - \max_j(r_{i,j}) + eq(o_i)$, where $eq(o_i)$ is the number of all equivalent objects to o_i.

Therefore, after initializing the heap H, the LRU-Buffer and the AuxB$^+$-tree, the main algorithmic process of both PBA1, PBA2 is the following.

- If H is empty then retrieve the next two common neighbor objects (by using a round-robin incremental nearest neighbor retrieval from the query objects), else only the next one, give them their estimated scores and insert them into H.

- Extract the top-1 object t_1 from H and if it has not an exact domination score then calculate it ($dom(t_1)$). Get also the top-2 object t_2 from H (without extraction and calculation).

- If $dom(t_1) \geq estdom(t_2)$ (or $dom(t_1) \geq dom(t_2)$ in case t_2 has an exact score), then report t_1 as the next top dominating result, else go to the first step.

- The process is repeated until all top-k dominating objects are reported.

For the exact domination score computation again the union property is used, thus: if t is a common neighbor object, and we count in $|U_t|$ all objects that have distances strictly smaller than t in the selected dimensions, and we also count in $|UE_t|$ all the equivalent objects to t, then it holds that: $dom(t) = N - |U_t| - |UE_t| - 1$.

To compute $|U_t|$ and $|UE_t|$, the algorithm PBA1 (similar with RA) scans backward into the nearest neighbor list of each query object, until the object t is detected. But PBA2 goes one step further. As all these objects are already retrieved and inserted into the AuxB$^+$-tree, the required counting can be successfully performed inside the AuxB$^+$-tree by using some additional counters, without materializing the sets U_t, UE_t and without scanning again the nearest neighbor lists.

The methodology of algorithms PBA1 and PBA2 enable the usage of several pruning heuristics, which reduce the runtime costs further. Three different types of pruning heuristics have been proposed: (i) Discard Heuristics – DH, which can discard objects that have not been retrieved yet; (ii) Early Pruning Heuristics – EPH, which can prune objects before the calculation of their exact domination scores; and (iii) an Internal Pruning Heuristic – IPH, which can prune objects during the procedure of the exact domination score calculation. For further details see Tiakas et al. (2014) and Tiakas et al. (2016).

4.7 TOP-*K* DOMINATING QUERIES IN OTHER ENVIRONMENTS

In Zhang et al. (2010a) there is a study of the problem of computing top-k dominating queries efficiently on uncertain data with a given probability threshold imposed to support different confidence requirements. A threshold-based probabilistic top-k dominating algorithm is proposed with an accuracy guarantee. Also an efficient randomized algorithm with an accuracy guarantee is proposed, which uses specific processing techniques and data structures (gCaR-trees).

In Kontaki et al. (2012) there is a first study of top-k dominating query processing algorithms in a streaming environment. Three exact algorithms (BFA, EVA, ADA) and two approximate algorithms that trade accuracy for speed (AHBA and AMSA) are proposed. AHBA offers probabilistic guarantees regarding the accuracy of the result based on the Hoeffding bound, whereas AMSA performs a more aggressive computation resulting in more efficient processing.

In Xie et al. (2013) there is a study of how to rank spatial objects with respect to their non-spatial attributes within their spatial neighborhoods. To enable a general ranking, a ranking function that inherits the advantages of domination relationship and integrates them with spatial proximity is used. The result is a top-k neighborhood domination query. An effective index structure, and a branch and bound algorithm that executes the ranking efficiently via the index is proposed.

In Han et al. (2015) there is a study for processing top-k dominating queries on massive data. The algorithm TDEP is proposed, which utilizes sorted lists built for each attribute with low cost to return top-k dominating results on massive data efficiently. TDEP divides the query processing in two phases: growing phase and shrinking phase. In each phase, TDEP retrieves the sorted lists in round-robin fashion and maintains the candidates until the stop condition is satisfied. Theoretical analysis is provided for the execution behavior of the two phases. The domination scores are computed only for the candidates that remain after the early pruning of TDEP.

In Amagata et al. (2016) there is a first study of top-k dominating query processing algorithms in distributed environments. An exact method for efficient top-k dominating data retrieval, which avoids redundant communication cost and latency, is proposed. Furthermore, an approximate version (variation of the exact method) is also proposed, which further reduces communication cost.

In Chen and Wang (2018) there is a study for top-k dominating query processing over distributed data streams. The proposed algorithm is based on Spark Streaming framework. Its main strategy is data partitioning and double pruning techniques (local and global), which can significantly reduce the number of candidate sets, reduce the computational overhead and space costs, and improve the query efficiency.

In Siddique et al. (2019) there is a study for efficient parallel algorithms for k-skyband queries and top-k dominating queries. An efficient method for computing both queries simultaneously in the parallel distributed framework MapReduce is proposed.

Finally, in Lai et al. (2019b) probabilistic top-k dominating query monitoring is studied over multiple uncertain IoT data streams in edge computing environments. An effective probabilistic top-k dominating query algorithm on uncertain data streams is proposed, which can be parallelized easily.

4.8 SUMMARY

In this chapter, we studied the top-k dominating queries, which combine the advantages of regular top-k and skyline queries, by bounding the size of the result without the need for user-defined scoring functions. They return to the user the k objects with the highest domination score, i.e., the number of other objects that dominate. In recent years, they became an active research area due to their importance in several modern applications.

We presented several efficient algorithms for top-k dominating query processing, covering index-based and index-free data, sub-spaces, metric spaces, and dynamic environments.

There is already a growing interest for studying top-k dominating queries in streaming environments, uncertain data, distributed environments, parallel computing platforms, and other interesting environments.

There are also many challenges for future work like: (i) approximate top-k dominating queries with approximation guarantees, which they trade accuracy for speed of computation; (ii) efficient processing of multiple top-k dominating queries in subsets of the data, or in multi-stream environments; and (iii) generate variations of the top-k dominating queries for specific models, environments and demanding applications.

CHAPTER 5

Applications of Dominance-Based Queries

In this chapter, we present various applications that are based on the dominance concept. There is actually a wide variety of applications that need dominance-based query processing facilities as fundamental building blocks in order to perform more complex operations. Some fields of applications include broad areas like Multi-Criteria Decision Making, Machine Learning, and Network Analysis but also more focused application domains like Online Medical Prognosis. In this chapter, we describe briefly some of these application domains and explain the way dominance is being used.

5.1   MULTI-CRITERIA DECISION MAKING

The skyline operator determines a set of points that are not dominated. In this sense, if we have to take a decision based on a specific dataset, the skyline points constitute good candidates to support our decision. Many of the applications that use the skyline or other variations of dominance-based queries in the recent literature, belong to the field of Multi-Criteria Decision Making and Quality of Service (QoS) evaluation.

5.1.1   SERVICE COMPOSITION

In this first example, the authors of Wang et al. (2020a) combine Reinforcement Learning (RL) with skyline computation and propose a method for service composition. The main idea of this study is to build an efficient process based on user-defined preference criteria. The result of this effort is the effective selection of services.

Assume that there is a service provider that proposes a travel plan based on user's preferences. The travel plan will include transportation and accommodation parameters. Each of these parameters may have various options, for example the transportation parameter may include the vehicles airplane, train, and ship, and each of the transportation options may have a number of services to choose. The services of the same option have the same attributes. For example, the airplane service will include response time, throughput, and reliability. When the skyline algorithm is applied, the number of candidates will be reduced and only services that are not dominated will remain. An example of service pruning is given in Figure 5.1.

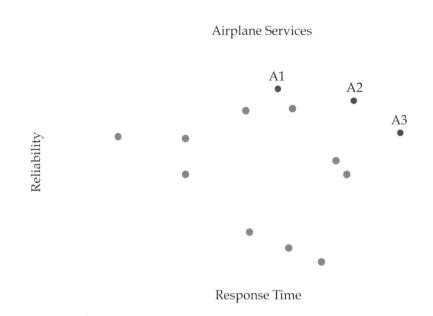

Figure 5.1: Airplane service pruning.

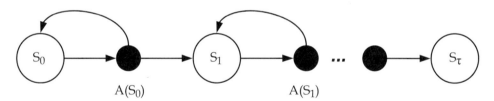

Figure 5.2: Service workflow model.

The process is represented as a Web Service Composition Markov Decision Process (WSC-MDP) model (see Figure 5.2). One part of the process uses RL to select the path that provides the most rewards, whereas the other part is used to lower the search space of the various candidates, which is done with the skyline computation.

5.1.2   WEB SERVICE SELECTION

The process of service selection can be a time-consuming process, if it follows the classic approach to compare the QoS (Quality of Service) attributes and then select the most suitable ones. In the work of Liang et al. (2019), the authors are using the skyline operator to select the best services based on QoS attributes. As noted in Liang et al. (2019), non-functional QoS attributes can be categorized to *cost-based attributes*, such as the price and service execution time, and *benefit-based attributes*, such as availability and reliability. The study proposes an improved skyline algorithm that filters and reduces the dominance checks, effectively. It also reduces the size of the service candidate set. This improves the efficiency of the service selection. The algorithm is evaluated with simulation and real-world data that verifies the high accuracy and efficiency of the proposed algorithm. The study suggests that in order to process massive data with the proposed algorithm, distributed frameworks should be used to improve execution.

5.1.3 RELIABILITY IN CLOUD COMPUTING

In the next example we review the work of Xiong et al. (2018) which belongs to the field of cloud computing. As the authors mention, cloud computing is gaining ground in information technology. The functional properties of cloud services are of high importance as they assure the correct functionality of the entire cloud application. At the same time, the nonfunctional properties, such as *reliability*, might have a considerable effect on the way the user perceives the quality of the application. Therefore, creating high-reliability cloud applications is a crucial research problem. Making the optimal cloud service selection from a set of functionally equivalent service candidates can be based on valuable information that is provided by reliability rankings. Several methods could conduct reliability ranking prediction of cloud services. Nevertheless, those methods did not resolve the skyline issue well, which is hard to be ranked. The authors in Xiong et al. (2018) proposed an approach to reliability ranking prediction for cloud services via skyline on the past service usage experiences of other consumers. Their approach keeps off costly and time-consuming Web service invocations. To validate their approach, the authors conducted large-scale experiments that were based on WSDream, a real-world Web service dataset (https://github.com/wsdream). The results showed that through their proposed approach higher prediction accuracy can be achieved compared to other approaches.

5.2 MACHINE LEARNING

5.2.1 INTRUSION DETECTION

One very interesting application that involves the skyline operator with Machine Learning and computer security is the work by Abdelkader et al. (2019). Intrusion detection systems (IDS) are critical in network security systems. These systems are mostly used to identify or to predict unauthorized activity. In order to minimize the threat, the system should minimize its alert misfire, either false negatives (true attacks that were not flagged) or false positives (activities that flagged incorrectly as attacks). Also, due to the fact that the alerts are possibly reviewed by a person, a high rate of false positive alerts will end up flooding the reviewer and increasing the chance of missing a real attack event.

Given this, intrusion detection can be distinguished into *anomaly detection* and *misuse detection*. Anomaly detection searches for attacks with known signatures, while misuse detection defines the normal behavior of the system and designates what is normal and abnormal behavior.

The proposed model, which is depicted in Figure 5.3, is constructed based on two levels. The first level contains the best classifiers with respect to accuracy, detection rate and false alert rate. The choice is made with the help of the skyline computation on three core criteria:

- maximize the accuracy,

- maximize the detection rate, and

- minimize the false alerts rate

The second level uses a Naive Bayesian classifier that incorporates the results of the first level and then takes the ultimate decision.

5.2.2   POLARITY CLASSIFICATION

In the work of Saidani et al. (2017) the idea of leveraging skyline computation in order to optimize the *feature selection* process for *polarity classification* was examined. Thus, a subset of Pareto optimal features that are not dominated by any other feature is allowed to be selected. One of the contributions of this paper, that relates to dominance-based queries, is that based on a set of metrics (or dimensions), a feature skyline is computed that significantly reduces the features space. In this way, irrelevant features are eliminated from the classification process.

In sentiment classification, the process of building the classification model consists of several steps. The first step involves the extraction of a set of features from the input data. Then, this set should be cleaned from irrelevant features. The cleaned feature set would then be ready to feed the learning algorithm and build the classification model, as shown in Figure 5.4.

The second step of the proposed method, reduces the number of features by using the skyline operator and select only those features that are most suitable in the process of building the classification model.

This idea is demonstrated with the following example. Given a database containing information about supposedly subjective words, for each word (term) the Term Frequency (tf), Relevance Frequency (rf), Term Frequency-Inverse Document Frequency (tf-idf), and Multinomial Z Score (zd) are stored.

The word with the largest rf and tf-idf is ideally what polarity classification is looking for. When the traditional skyline is applied on the word list in Table 5.1, the terms "Good" and "Bad" are returned (see Figure 5.5), which can be considered as the most relevant terms.

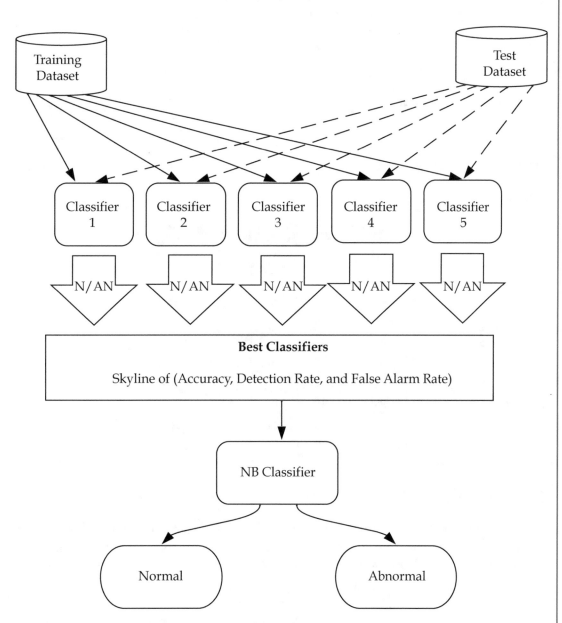

Figure 5.3: Proposed naive Bayesian classifier model.

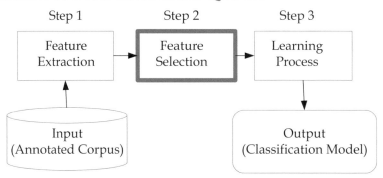

Figure 5.4: Classification process.

Table 5.1: List of words

Term	tf	rf	tf-idf	zd
Wrong	32	5	10	35
Superior	41	7	5	19
Correct	37	5	12	45
Like	36	4	11	39
Bad	40	8	10	18
Actors	30	4	6	27
Tonight	31	3	4	56
Good	36	6	13	12
Hope	33	6	6	95
Inferior	40	7	9	20

5.3   NETWORK ANALYSIS

Networks are everywhere! Due to their great ability to model interactions among entities they are being used in many application domains. In this section we review some important applications that require the use of dominance to apply network analysis.

5.3.1   GRAPH CLUSTERING

In Dhifli et al. (2020), a graph clustering approach is proposed for mining clusters over large attributed graphs based on the dominance relationship. Each skyline solution is optimized simultaneously for multiple fitness functions, and each function is defined over the graph topology or over a particular set of attributes derived from multiple data sources.

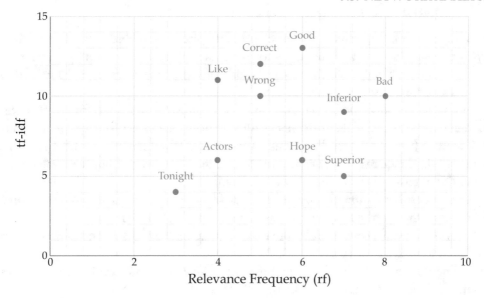

Figure 5.5: Skyline of the features.

The proposed approach is evaluated experimentally with a large protein-protein inter-action network of the human interactome[1] enriched with large sets of heterogeneous cancer-associated attributes. The authors of Dhifli et al. (2020) noted that their approach can be summarized as follows.

- First, disjoint powerset systems are constructed from possible combinations of nodes to form potential candidate graph clusters.

- A set of chromosomes is then constructed with a personalized initialization algorithm that favors the density and connectivity of the initial candidate clustering solutions.

- Personalized genetic operators are then used on the first population to generate new optimized chromosomes iteratively. These new chromosomes are then evaluated, using multiple objective functions defined over the graph topology and the node and/or edge attributes. Encoding and decoding functions are also defined to map the contents of the chromosomes to their respective sets (i.e., candidate clusters) in the corresponding powerset system.

After repeating this process for a predefined number of iterations, a set of approximate non-dominated graph clustering solutions based on the skyline operator is obtained.

---

[1]Interactome: the whole set of molecular interactions in a particular cell.

5.3.2 GRAPH COMMUNITY SEARCH

Community search is a query-dependent community discovery problem. Because of the large number of applications the topic has attracted much attention. The community search problem can be seen as a problem in which we try to find densely connected subgraphs in a network, based on a specific query.

In a social networks, nodes are associated with numerical attributes. These attributes can be obtained form the metadata of the nodes directly or form another source such as a network analysis method (e.g., the degree, PageRank, influence, etc.). In this context, when given a multi-valued network, the question is how to find the communities that are not dominated by other communities in terms of their numerical attributes.

To answer this question, the reviewed study of Li et al. (2018) propose a novel community model called skyline community and its based on the concept of skyline and k-core. A skyline community is a maximal connected k-core that is not dominated by other connected k-cores in the d-dimensional attribute space.

The authors of Li et al. (2018) propose the *skyline community model* which defines the domination relationship between two communities as follows.

Let $H = (V_H, E_H)$ be an induced subgraph of G, the value of H in the x_i dimension is defined as:

$$f_i(H) = \min_{v \in V_H} \{x_i^v\}.$$

Definition 5.1 Let $H = (V_H, E_H)$ and $H' = (V_{H'}, E_{H'})$ be two communities. If $f_i(H) \leq f_i(H')$ for all $i = 1, \ldots, d$ and there exists $f_i(H) < f_i(H')$ for a certain i, we call that H' dominates H, denoted by $H \prec H'$.

Definition 5.2 Given a multi-valued graph $G = (V, E, X)$ and an integer k. A skyline community with a parameter k is an induced subgraph $H = (V_H, E_H, X_H)$ of G such that it satisfies the following properties:

- cohesive property: H is a k-core (i.e., H is a connected k-core);

- skyline property: there does not exist an induced subgraph H' of G such that H' is a k-core and $H \prec H'$; and

- maximal property: there does not exist an induced subgraph H' of G such that (i) H' is a k-core, (ii) H' contains H, and (iii) $f_i(H') = f_i(H)$ for all $i = 1, \ldots, d$.

Based on the above definitions, Figure 5.6 depicts an example of how the skyline communities are formed. In this example, there are two skyline communities, $H_1 = \{v_1, v_2, v_3\}$ (by Definition 5.2) and similarly $H_2 = \{v_2, v_4, v_5, v_6\}$. The subgraph $H_3 = \{v_4, v_5, v_6\}$ and $H_4 = \{v_2, v_3, v_4, v_5, v_6\}$ are not skyline communities because H_3 has the same f values as H_2

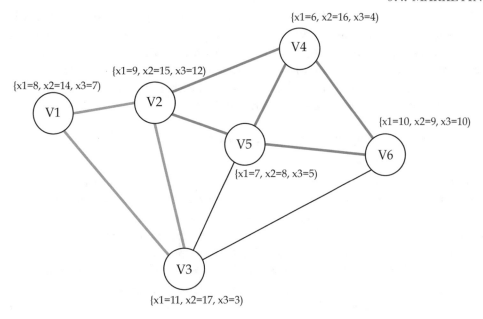

Figure 5.6: Skyline community search example for 2-core.

and also it is contained in H_2. The subgraph H_4 is also not a skyline community because it is dominated by H_1 and H_2.

5.4   MARKETING

To find products online, users are searching and ranking items based on specific criteria, for example in the case of searching to buy a laptop, typical features include the amount of memory, CPU specifications, battery type and so on. All these ranking queries are implemented with the help of a top-k algorithm. In this section we will review three papers where these kind of queries are used to exploit the market and provide valuable information to the manufacturer this time, to produce new or improve an existing product in order to maximize his profitability and allow his products to be ranked among the top-k.

5.4.1   TARGETING A GENERAL GROUP OF BUYERS

From the point of the manufacturer, placing a new product to the market having a specific target group of potential buyers is something that every business owner keeps in mind. The problem here is how to place this new option to the market, in a way that it ranks in the top-k of any user in the target group. Another possible scenario is that an existing product needs to be improved by modifying its features, in order to appear in the k-top ranking results in a specific user group, and also that modification will require the minimum possible cost. The paper by Tang et al.

(2019) deals with this problem. It is the first work on competitive option placement where no distinct user(s) are targeted, but a general clientele type. The paper introduces the top-ranking region problem (TopRR) that computes the maximal region oR in option space in which any option o will rank among the top-k for every weight vector in a target preference region wR. The authors propose a test-and-split solution combined with extra optimizations and show how effective and practical it is on large benchmark datasets.

5.4.2   PRODUCT FEATURE SELECTION TO MAXIMIZE PROFITABILITY

The optimization problem, presented in Ge et al. (2015), tries to find the features of a new product to maximize its profitability, given a set of products that are modeled by their feature values. Here the profitability is modeled by the number of products which dominate and are dominated by the new product. The search space is constrained by the available budget, which is monotone to the feature values. By assuming this, the problem becomes a set of continuous regions in the feature space, that can be accurately expressed by minimum bounding rectangles (MBRs) according to the authors. The paper proposes three methods to approach this problem and compares them. The first baseline method, which has exponential time and space complexity regarding dimensionality, iteratively processes the existing products and refines regions in space enclosing feasible feature vectors with the same profitability bounds. The second method proposed, uses depth-first search in a divide-and-conquer (D&C) approach while the third method is a hybrid method that applies best-first search in the D&C framework. The experiments show that the last two methods scale much better than the baseline approach. The authors also propose an approximation method based on the D&C strategy and show that this method can find a result of one percent or less relative difference to the optimal much faster than exact approach.

5.4.3   EFFECTIVE PRODUCT POSITIONING

The authors of Li et al. (2006a) introduce, for the first time, the concept of dominance from a micro-economic standpoint that has application in business analysis. This new form of analysis is called Dominant Relationship Analysis (DRA). To illustrate the various aspect of this new form of analysis the authors propose three types of queries, Linear Optimization Query (LOQ), Subspace Analysis Query (SAQ), and Comparative Dominant Query (CDQ). All three types of queries are using the also proposed novel data cube called DADA (Data Cube for Dominant Relationship Analysis). According to the authors, DRA is used to provide insight into the dominant relationships between products and potential buyers. By analyzing such relationships, companies can position their products more effectively while remaining profitable. The DADA cube is essentially used to summarize all the domination relationships between objects in all dimensions. The authors also propose the D*-tree, a data structure to search efficiently and answer all three Dominant Relationship Queries (DRQ).

5.5   HEALTHCARE

In this section we will see two applications which are in the field of healthcare.

5.5.1   ONLINE PRIMARY DIAGNOSIS

The first example is about a medical prognosis system called CINEMA. In particular, an efficient and privacy-preserving online medical primary diagnosis has been proposed in Hua et al. (2019). The proposed system offer a precise diagnosis with the use of skyline computation in the medical data. CINEMA also takes into account the security and privacy issues that may arise. The system allow users to perform a privacy-preserving primary medical diagnosis by their own, based on the diagnosis model which is located at the service provider. The service provider on the other hand allows this diagnosis without revealing the disease diagnosis model.

In general, CINEMA consist of five phases:

1. System initialization

2. Data preparation

3. Query generation

4. Privacy-preserving online medical primary diagnosis service

5. Query result reading

As we can see in Figure 5.7, the system is structured in such a way to protected the user medical data. The skyline computation is used here as a tool for the diagnosis.

The service provider, which is usually a healthcare center/hospital, owns a skyline diagnosis model which consist of two parts. Positive skyline point set PSKY(P) and negative skyline point set NSKY(P). Each point in the dataset contains a number of attributes such as age in years, resting blood pressure in mm/Hg, serum cholesterol in mg/dl, fasting blood sugar, and so on. When a user query enters the system, the query point has to be dominated both positive and negative in order for the diagnosis to be positive.

A positive domination relationship is defined as:

$$\mathrm{Pdom}(P_a, P_b) = \begin{cases} 1, & \text{if } P_a \text{ positive dominated } P_b \\ 0, & \text{otherwise,} \end{cases}$$

and a negative as:

$$\mathrm{Ndom}(P_a, P_b) = \begin{cases} -1, & \text{if } P_a \text{ negative dominated } P_b \\ 0, & \text{otherwise .} \end{cases}$$

The diagnosis model then is defined as:

$$\begin{cases} \rho_+ = \frac{1}{s} \sum_{i=1}^{s} \mathrm{Pdom}(\vec{a}_i, \vec{w}) \\ \rho_- = \frac{1}{t} \sum_{j=1}^{t} \mathrm{Ndom}(\vec{b}_j, \vec{w}). \end{cases}$$

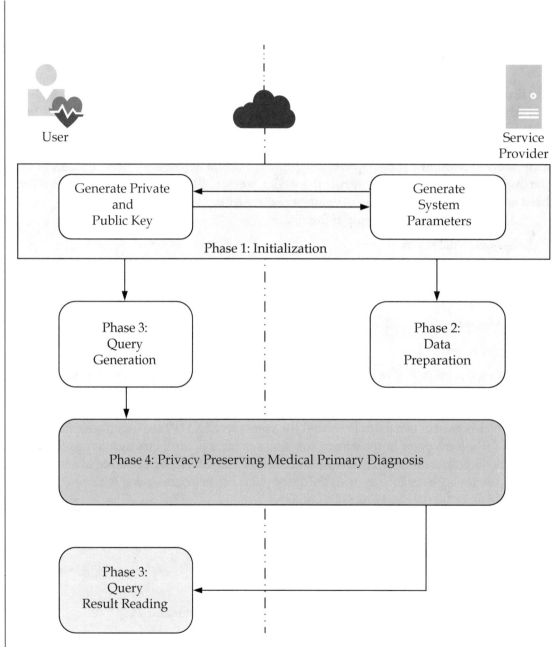

Figure 5.7: Architecture of CINEMA.

If $\rho_+ = 1$ and $\rho_- = -1$ then the diagnosis is positive.

5.5.2   OVER-TREATMENT REDUCTION

In the second example from Che et al. (2018), the authors are proposing a practical approach to reduce over-treatment in hospitals. The medical data of the patients are modeled as a multidimensional set in order to provide advice for doctors and patients.

By using valuable historical data in Hospital Information System, the authors used an approach to identify and analyze treatment cases with low fees, and then selected these cases to recommend to patients and doctors. On the other hand, over-treatment cases can also be identified and used as examples of treatments to avoid.

The proposed solution considers inpatients and outpatients as different situations and uses different number of measures for each case. To identify the appropriate treatment data the historical medical data need to be sorted. In each case, a different strategy is followed. For inpatients five measures are considered while in the outpatients case only two. The difference in dimensionality for the two cases has lead the authors to solve the problem separately. For the case of the inpatients, due to fact that the dimensionality is higher, a top-k dominant skyline operator has been used, which can efficiently sort data in high dimensional space. On the 2-dimensional case of the outpatients, the basic skyline operator was used. Figure 5.8 shows the proposed system.

5.6   OTHER INTERESTING APPLICATIONS

In this section we discuss briefly applications from additional domains, including Image Retrieval, Scientometrics, Chemical Process Monitoring, Wireless Routing, Sensor Selection, E-Commerce, and Indoor Route Search. In addition, we discuss how dominance-based queries can be supported by Database Management Systems.

5.6.1   IMAGE RETRIEVAL

The first example is an image retrieval application from Georgiadis et al. (2019). Here the skyline is used to exploit the natural properties of images. Images are usually transformed into *feature vectors* or *descriptor vectors*, which encode the most important image characteristics into a simple vector representation. These vectors are usually of high dimensionality, ranging from a few tens to hundreds or even thousands, depending on the transformation of feature extraction technique applied on the raw data. The resulting vector contains only part of the information that the original image have, for example color information, shape, texture, or a combination thereof.

The intrinsic dissimilarities of images can be captured by finding the skyline using their descriptor vectors, thus, dissimilar images are detected without defining any similarity or distance function. A concrete application of this study is that images found in the skyline can be used as seeds for grouping or clustering the images of the whole image collection with respect to their similarity. The proposed method combines several skyline methods with four state-of-

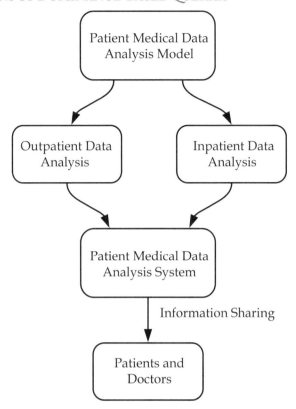

Figure 5.8: Medical analysis system.

the-art hashing algorithms for data partitioning and indexing efficiency in secondary memory to support scalability. Figure 5.9 depicts the proposed model.

In the clustering evaluation, the outcome of two basic clustering algorithms are compared in order to measure the distance and similarity of the cluster centers initially when the algorithm is initiated randomly, compared to the case when the algorithm is initiated by the skyline items. The study concluded to the fact that when skyline items are used as seeds, cluster centers are close and similar to the centers from random initialization. Additionally, in the current evaluation, a quicker convergence of the clustering has been observed when the algorithm is initiated with the skyline items.

5.6.2 SCIENTOMETRICS

In an attempt to state the quantitative and qualitative characteristics of scientific output, a variety of scientometric indices has been proposed. Nevertheless, as each proposed index focuses solely on specific features of scientific performance, fully capturing the performance and im-

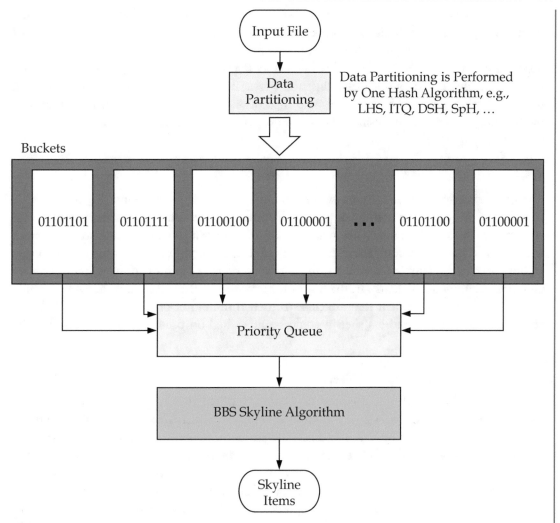

Figure 5.9: Hash BBS skyline process.

pact of a scientific entity (author, journal, institution, etc.) is a research issue yet to be studied. Additionally, in the study of Sidiropoulos et al. (2016) it is noted that despite the plethora of scientometric indices proposed to rank scientists, none of them can fully capture the performance and impact of a scientist, since each index quantifies only one or a few aspects of his/her multifarious performance. As a result, scientific evaluation can be perceived as a multi-dimensional ranking problem, where dimensions stand for the diverse scientometric indices. To address this problem, the skyline operator has been proposed in Sidiropoulos et al. (2016) with multiple combinations of dimensions.

In Stoupas et al. (2018), a new index deriving from the use of the skyline operator, called Rainbow Ranking or RR-index was presented. This index does not produce a strict ordering of the ranked entities. It assigns a category score to every scientific entity. The presented RR-index, depending on the purposes of the evaluation, allows the combination of any known indices and outputs a single number metric expressing multi-criteria relative ranking. It can also be applied to any scientific entity such as journals and institutions. The authors evaluated the proposed methodology experimentally using a dataset of over 105,000 scientists from the Computer Science field.

5.6.3   MONITOR OF CHEMICAL PROCESS

The application described in the next example is from the chemical process industry. In the paper by Wang et al. (2016a), a method is proposed to monitor the running condition of chemical equipment. The system contains a wireless sensor network, which collects measurements from the current chemical process. The data are collected and stored in a distributed environment. In order to detect a fault in the process, the authors propose a monitor strategy that can detect abnormal equipment efficiently. In the heart of the process, is the dynamic skyline query which is used to identify equipment that are close to their threshold of possible explosion. When a condition like this is identified then it could be prevented on time. Figure 5.10 displays the monitor process.

5.6.4   WIRELESS ROUTING

In Yakine et al. (2016), the skyline operator is used to efficiently route the communication between a wireless Ad-Hoc Network. A wireless Ad-Hoc Network is able to communicate without the need of infrastructure or centralized administration. The purpose of an Ad-Hoc Network is to provide communication between it's nodes which are both end-points and routing nodes. If the communication is about to happen between nodes that are not directly connected then it must be done through an intermediate node. This dynamic nature of the network is forcing each node to take single-hop decisions. The proposed method is using the skyline computation to find routes in a wireless network that respect QoS parameters like hop count, delay, bandwidth, and cost.

5.6.5   SENSOR SELECTION

The data generated by the IoT sensors are available to be used from other IoT systems. The challenge is to select from a very large number of sensors those that are most appropriate to the user's requirements. In Kertiou et al. (2018), the authors are dealing with this problem. The following example illustrates the proposed solution. It is assumed that there are three gateways G1, G2, G3, and each gateway manages a number of sensors. The sensors have attributes like ID, locality, type, accuracy, reliability, and cost. Each sensor has a distinct set of values for these attributes. When a user requests a certain type of sensor, the following actions are performed.

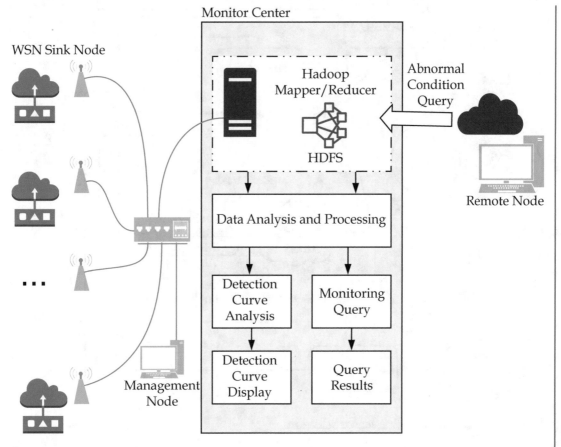

Figure 5.10: Monitor process.

1. The server receives the request.

2. Each gateway computes the local dynamic skyline based on user requirements.

3. The server receives the dynamic skylines and merges them into one global dynamic skyline.

4. The user applies the weights for each of the proximity-based requirements and the values of the sensors are displayed to the user ranked.

   The above example is depicted in Figure 5.11.

5.6.6   E-COMMERCE

In e-Commerce, the skyline query can be seen as a tool to help the customer to choose between products. The problem that the authors in Zhou et al. (2019) are trying to solve is a *constrained*

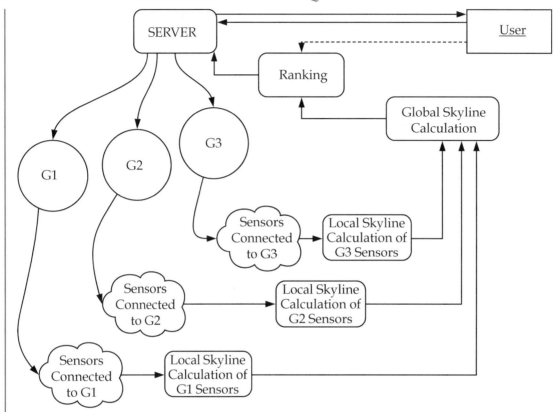

Figure 5.11: Dynamic skyline sensor selection.

optimal product combination (COPC) problem. The idea is to find out the skyline product combinations which the customer is willing to buy and that have maximum discount rate. The authors firstly propose a two-list exact (TLE) algorithm to process the problem effectively. This approach is suitable only for small datasets. It does not scale well because it requires to process an exponential number of product combinations, as the problem is proved by this study to be NP-hard. Additionally to the TLE algorithm, the authors propose a lower-bound approximate (LBA) algorithm that has a guarantee about the accuracy of the results and an incremental greedy (IG) algorithm that has good performance. The study verifies the significance of the COPC problem by conducting a customer study and shows the effectiveness of the proposed algorithms with an experimental evaluation based on real-world and synthetic datasets.

5.6.7 INDOOR ROUTE SEARCH

The following application is trying to solve the problem of route planning in an indoor venue. The authors of Salgado (2018) are using the skyline query to find routes that are not dominated. The study proposes a new route searching problem called *keyword-aware skyline routes* (KSR) query. The difference with traditional route planning queries is that KSR considers also the number of stores the proposed route should contain, while the traditional route planing is selecting the optimal route with respect to distance/time. For example, a user is visiting a large shopping center and wants to buy three items. If the user issues a traditional route planning query that returns the optimal route w.r.t distance/time, then she may receive a plan that is directing her to go to three different shops. But waiting in three counters could result in more waiting time than to buy all three items from one store. Thus, taking into account also the number of stores a route is visiting, is a parameter to consider to find an optimal route. The authors of Salgado (2018) propose an exact algorithm to answer KSR queries. While the problem is shown to be NP-hard, if the number of keywords is small, which is the typical case, then the peoposed solution is efficient.

5.7   DATABASE SUPPORT FOR DOMINANCE QUERIES

In the previous sections we have seen how dominance queries are being used by several interesting application domains. In this section, we provide a few details regarding the support of dominance-based queries in database management systems (DBMSs). Since in most of the cases an application is supported by a database management system, it is interesting to see how dominance-based query processing techniques are implemented.

The algorithmic techniques described in the previous chapters guarantee that dominance-based queries will run efficiently. However, the implementation of these techniques at the core of a DBMS system requires significant attention. In general, there are two different techniques that may be followed (Levandoski et al., 2010):

- the *on-top* approach, which suggests that any preference computation is decoupled from the database by either implementing them as an external standalone application or as a user-defined function; and

- the *built-in* approach, which deals with the implementation of preference computation at the core of the DBMS.

The difficulty in implementing new features at the heart of the DBMS has the consequence that usually, there is a large period of time between the invention of new database techniques and their adoption by the database industry toward their implementation in commercial systems or research prototypes. This is because the integration of new techniques and their implementation deep inside the DBMS involves several other changes that in many cases are difficult to perform and guarantee efficiency. The built-in approach, although it requires significantly more efforts to implement, offers many advantages since the preference evaluation is coupled with other primitive database operations like search, joins, and aggregations.

First, let us discuss how dominance-based queries can be expressed using SQL extensions. Extending SQL is one of the most important issues toward supporting new functionality in database management systems. In the seminal work of Börzsönyi et al. (2001), the skyline query is supported by extending SQL with the SKYLINE OF operator. The general form of the clause is as follows:

```
SELECT ... FROM ... WHERE ...
GROUP BY ... HAVING ...
SKYLINE OF [DISTINCT] a1 [MIN|MAX|DIFF], ..., am [MIN|MAX|DIFF]
ORDER BY ...
```

In the above clause, MIN, MAX, and DIFF refer to each attribute a_i participating in the skyline, standing for maximum, minimum, and different values. This way, the user may pose preferences for each attribute separately. Evidently, the output of the SKYLINE OF clause comprises all database records (a.k.a. tuples) that are not dominated based on the preferences expressed by the user. Note also that the SKYLINE OF operator must be evaluated after SELECT, FROM, WHERE, and GROUP BY, HAVING but before ORDER BY.

In addition to the skyline operator, there are several proposals to incorporate preference-based query processing in a DBMS (Carey and Kossmann, 1997; Fagin et al., 2001). Taking into account that preference queries may take many different forms, it is not practical to support dominance-based queries by performing ad-hoc changes to the DBMS engine every time a new query is invented. To overcome this problem, the FlexPref framework (Levandoski et al., 2010) has been proposed, which constitutes a generalized solution to incorporate difference preferences. This framework suggests that in order to support different kinds of preferences, the following functions need to be implemented, where p and q are objects and S is a set of objects.

- *PairwiseCompare*(p, q). Returns 1 if q can never be a preferred object, -1 if p can never be a preferred object, and 0 otherwise.

- *IsPreferredObject*(p, S). Returns 1 if p is a preferred object and can be added to S, -1 otherwise.

- *AddPreferredToSet*(p, S). Inserts p to S and removes or rearranges objects from S, if necessary.

The great innovation of FlexPref is that by using the aforementioned functions, there is no need to be aware of details about the way query processing is being implemented. In Levandoski et al. (2010) the authors demonstrate how this framework can be used for primitive database operations like table access, joins, and sorted list access as well as preference-based queries such as top-k, skyline, k-dominance, and top-k dominance. Moreover, the FlexPref framework has been implemented in the PostgreSQL DBMS and it has been evaluated experimentally, paving the way for the implementation of dominance-based operators in commercial database systems.

5.8   SUMMARY

In this chapter, we presented applications from various fields that require the use of dominance-based queries. The basic field of application is Multi-Criteria Decision Making which is a straightforward application of the skyline operator. We also reviewed applications related to Machine Learning, IoT, Network Analytics, and Healthcare. Moreover, we have presented some additional interesting applications from various fields including Image Retrieval, Scientometrics, Process Monitoring, Wireless Routing, and E-Commerce. Finally, we discussed briefly how dominance-based queries can be supported at the core of database management systems.

The wide range of applications shows the significance but also the usefulness of the skyline and related queries. The skyline operator is applied naturally in multidimensional data and helps to understand and discover points of interest, but it can also be applied to more sophisticated management or analysis tasks.

Bibliography

Alem Abdelkader, Youcef Dahmani, and Bendaoud Bendaoud. Skyline computation for improving naïve Bayesian classifier in intrusion detection system. *Ingénierie des Systèmes d'Information*, 24(5):513–518, 2019. https://doi.org/10.18280/isi.240508 93

Foto N. Afrati, Paraschos Koutris, Dan Suciu, and Jeffrey D. Ullman. Parallel skyline queries. *Theory of Computing Systems*, 57(4):1008–1037, 2015. DOI: 10.1007/s00224-015-9627-3 60

Karim Alami, Nicolas Hanusse, Patrick Kamnang Wanko, and Sofian Maabout. The negative skycube. *Information Systems*, 88, 2020. DOI: 10.1016/j.is.2019.101443 42

Daichi Amagata, Yuya Sasaki, Takahiro Hara, and Shojiro Nishio. Efficient processing of top-k dominating queries in distributed environments. *World Wide Web*, 19:545–577, 2016. DOI: 10.1007/s11280-015-0340-6 90

Wolf-Tilo Balke, Ulrich Güntzer, and Jason Xin Zheng. Efficient distributed skylining for web information systems. In *Proc. of the 9th International Conference on Extending Database Technology (EDBT)*, pages 256–273, 2004. DOI: 10.1007/978-3-540-24741-8_16 20, 27

Suman Banerjee and Bithika Pal. DySky: Dynamic skyline queries on uncertain graphs. *CoRR*, 2020. https://arxiv.org/abs/2004.02564 45

Ilaria Bartolini, Paolo Ciaccia, and Marco Patella. Salsa: Computing the skyline without scanning the whole sky. In *Proc. of the 15th ACM International Conference on Information and Knowledge Management (CIKM)*, pages 405–414, 2006. DOI: 10.1145/1183614.1183674 17

Jon Louis Bentley, H. T. Kung, Mario Schkolnick, and Clark D. Thompson. On the average number of maxima in a set of vectors and applications. *Journal of the ACM*, 25(4):536–543, 1978. DOI: 10.1145/322092.322095 33

Kenneth S. Bøgh, Sean Chester, Darius Sidlauskas, and Ira Assent. Hashcube: A data structure for space-and query-efficient skycube compression. In *Proc. of the 23rd ACM International Conference on Information and Knowledge Management (CIKM)*, pages 1767–1770, 2014. DOI: 10.1145/2661829.2661891 42

Kenneth S. Bøgh, Sean Chester, Darius Šidlauskas, and Ira Assent. Template skycube algorithms for heterogeneous parallelism on multicore and GPU architectures. In *Proc. of the ACM International Conference on Management of Data (SIGMOD)*, pages 447–462, 2017. DOI: 10.1145/3035918.3035962 42

Christian Buchta. On the average number of maxima in a set of vectors. *Information Processing Letters*, 33(2):63–65, 1989. DOI: 10.1016/0020-0190(89)90156-7 33

Stephan Börzsönyi, Donald Kossmann, and Konrad Stocker. The skyline operator. In *Proc. of the 17th IEEE International Conference on Data Engineering (ICDE)*, pages 421–430, 2001. DOI: 10.1109/icde.2001.914855 6, 14, 15, 17, 20, 21, 34, 44, 110

Michael J. Carey and Donald Kossmann. On saying "enough already!" in sql. *SIGMOD*, pages 219–230, Association for Computing Machinery, New York, 1997. DOI: 10.1145/253260.253302. 110

Chee Yong Chan, Pin-Kwang Eng, and Kian-Lee Tan. Stratified computation of skylines with partially-ordered domains. In *Proc. of the ACM International Conference on Management of Data (SIGMOD)*, pages 203–214, 2005. DOI: 10.1145/1066157.1066181 60

Chee Yong Chan, H. V. Jagadish, Kian-Lee Tan, Anthony K. H. Tung, and Zhenjie Zhang. Finding t-dominant skylines in high dimensional space. In *Proc. of the ACM International Conference on Management of Data (SIGMOD)*, pages 503–514, 2006. DOI: 10.1145/1142473.1142530 38, 39

Min Che, Liya Wang, and Zhibin Jiang. An approach to multidimensional medical data analysis based on the skyline operator. In *Proc. of the IEEE International Conference on Industrial Engineering and Engineering Management (IEEM)*, pages 1806–1810, 2018. DOI: 10.1109/ieem.2018.8607324 103

Guidan Chen and Yongheng Wang. Top-k dominating query processing over distributed data streams. *Global Journal of Engineering Science and Research Management*, 5(6):13–24, 2018. http://www.gjesrm.com/Issues%20PDF/Archive-2018/June-2018/3.pdf 90

Lei Chen and Xiang Lian. Efficient processing of metric skyline queries. *IEEE Transactions on Knowledge and Data Engineering*, 21(3):351–365, 2009. DOI: 10.1109/tkde.2008.146 51, 52, 53

Lijiang Chen, Bin Cui, and Hua Lu. Constrained skyline query processing against distributed data sites. *IEEE Transactions on Knowledge and Data Engineering*, 23(2):204–217, 2011. DOI: 10.1109/tkde.2010.103 55

Yi-Chung Chen and Chiang Lee. The σ-neighborhood skyline queries. *Information Sciences*, 322:92–114, 2015. DOI: 10.1016/j.ins.2015.06.015 61

Jan Chomicki, Parke Godfrey, Jarek Gryz, and Dongming Liang. Skyline with presorting: Theory and optimizations. In *Proc. of the International Conference on Intelligent Information Processing and Web Mining (IIPWM)*, pages 595–604, 2005. DOI: 10.1007/3-540-32392-9_72 15, 16, 41, 57

Jan Chomicki, Paolo Ciaccia, and Niccolo' Meneghetti. Skyline queries, front and back. *ACM SIGMOD Record*, 42(3):6–18, 2013. DOI: 10.1145/2536669.2536671 6

Paolo Ciaccia, Marco Patella, and Pavel Zezula. M-tree: An efficient access method for similarity search in metric spaces. In *Proc. of the 23rd International Conference on Very Large Data Bases (VLDB)*, pages 426–435, 1997. http://www.vldb.org/conf/1997/P426.PDF 84, 88

Douglas Comer. Ubiquitous B-tree. *ACM Computing Surveys*, 11(2):121–137, 1979. DOI: 10.1145/356770.356776 20

Indraneel Das and John E. Dennis. Normal-boundary intersection: A new method for generating the pareto surface in nonlinear multicriteria optimization problems. *SIAM Journal on Optimization*, 8(3):631–657, 1998. DOI: 10.1137/s1052623496307510 6

Evangelos Dellis and Bernhard Seeger. Efficient computation of reverse skyline queries. In *Proc. of the 33rd International Conference on Very Large Data Bases (VLDB)*, pages 291–302, 2007. http://www.vldb.org/conf/2007/papers/research/p291-dellis.pdf 60

Ke Deng, Xiaofang Zhou, and Heng Tao Shen. Multi-source skyline query processing in road networks. In *Proc. of the 23rd IEEE International Conference on Data Engineering (ICDE)*, pages 796–805, 2007. DOI: 10.1109/icde.2007.367925 47

Wajdi Dhifli, Nour El Islem Karabadji, and Mohamed Elati. Evolutionary mining of skyline clusters of attributed graph data. *Information Sciences*, 509:501–514, 2020. DOI: 10.1016/j.ins.2018.09.053 96, 97

Linlin Ding, Shu Wang, Xiao Zhang, and Baoyan Song. Efficient k-dominant skyline query based on dominate hierarchical tree in MapReduce. In *Proc. of the 14th International Conference on Natural Computation, Fuzzy Systems and Knowledge Discovery (ICNC-FSKD)*, pages 933–939, 2018. DOI: 10.1109/fskd.2018.8687292 40

Ahmed K. Elmagarmid, Panagiotis G. Ipeirotis, and Vassilios S. Verykios. Duplicate record detection: A survey. *IEEE Transactions on Knowledge and Data Engineering*, 19(1):1–16, 2006. DOI: 10.1109/tkde.2007.250581 52

Ronald Fagin. Combining fuzzy information from multiple systems. In *Proc. of the 15th ACM Symposium on Principles of Database Systems (PODS)*, pages 216–226, 1996. DOI: 10.1145/237661.237715 2, 20

Ronald Fagin, Amnon Lotem, and Moni Naor. Optimal aggregation algorithms for middleware. *PODS*, pages 102–113, Association for Computing Machinery, New York, 2001. https://doi.org/10.1145/375551.375567 110

Marta Fort, Joan Antoni Sellarès, and Nacho Valladares. Nearest and farthest spatial skyline queries under multiplicative weighted Euclidean distances. *Knowledge-Based Systems*, 192, 2020. DOI: 10.1016/j.knosys.2019.105299 48

Xiaoyi Fu, Xiaoye Miao, Jianliang Xu, and Yunjun Gao. Continuous range-based skyline queries in road networks. *World Wide Web*, 20(6):1443–1467, 2017. DOI: 10.1007/s11280-017-0444-2 57

David Fuhry, Ruoming Jin, and Donghui Zhang. Efficient skyline computation in metric space. In *Proc. of the 12th International Conference on Extending Database Technology (EDBT)*, pages 1042–1051, 2009. DOI: 10.1145/1516360.1516479 53, 86

Yunjun Gao, Gencai Chen, Ling Chen, and Chun Chen. Parallelizing progressive computation for skyline queries in multi-disk environment. In *Proc. of the 17th International Conference on Database and Expert Systems Applications (DEXA)*, pages 697–706, 2006. DOI: 10.1007/11827405_68 60

Yunjun Gao, Qing Liu, Baihua Zheng, and Gang Chen. On efficient reverse skyline query processing. *Expert Systems with Applications*, 41(7):3237–3249, 2014a. DOI: 10.1016/j.eswa.2013.11.012 60

Yunjun Gao, Xiaoye Miao, Huiyong Cui, Gang Chen, and Qing Li. Processing *k*-skyband, constrained skyline, and group-by skyline queries on incomplete data. *Expert Systems with Applications*, 41(10):4959–4974, 2014b. DOI: 10.1016/j.eswa.2014.02.033 60

Shen Ge, Leong Hou U, Nikos Mamoulis, and David Wai-Lok Cheung. Dominance relationship analysis with budget constraints. *Knowledge and Information Systems*, 42(2):409–440, 2015. DOI: 10.1007/s10115-013-0694-y 100

Nikolaos Georgiadis, Eleftherios Tiakas, Yannis Manolopoulos, and Apostolos N. Papadopoulos. Skyline-based dissimilarity of images. *Journal of Intelligent Information Systems*, 53(3):509–545, 2019. DOI: 10.1007/s10844-019-00571-y 103

Parke Godfrey. Skyline cardinality for relational processing. In *Proc. of the 3rd International Symposium on Foundations of Information and Knowledge Systems (FoIKS)*, pages 78–97, 2004. DOI: 10.1007/978-3-540-24627-5_7 33

Parke Godfrey, Ryan Shipley, and Jarek Gryz. Maximal vector computation in large data sets. In *Proc. of the 31st International Conference on Very Large Data Bases (VLDB)*, pages 229–240, 2005. http://www.vldb.org/archives/website/2005/program/paper/tue/p229-godfrey.pdf 16

Marlene Goncalves and Leonid Tineo. Fuzzy dominance skyline queries. In *Proc. of the 18th International Conference on Database and Expert Systems Applications (DEXA)*, pages 469–478, 2007. DOI: 10.1007/978-3-540-74469-6_46 60

Xi Guo, Yoshiharu Ishikawa, and Yunjun Gao. Direction-based spatial skylines. In *Proc. of the 9th ACM International Workshop on Data Engineering for Wireless and Mobile Access (Mobide)*, pages 73–80, 2010. DOI: 10.1145/1850822.1850835 49, 50

Antonin Guttman. R-trees: A dynamic index structure for spatial searching. In *Proc. of the ACM International Conference on Management of Data (SIGMOD)*, pages 47–57, 1984. DOI: 10.1145/602259.602266 14, 21, 66

Xixian Han, Jianzhong Li, and Hong Gao. TDEP: efficiently processing top-k dominating query on massive data. *Knowledge and Information Systems*, 43(3):689–718, 2015. DOI: 10.1007/s10115-013-0728-5 89

Xixian Han, Bailing Wang, and Guojun Lai. Dynamic skyline computation on massive data. *Knowledge and Information Systems*, 59(3):571–599, 2019. DOI: 10.1007/s10115-018-1193-y 44

Guoliang He, Lu Chen, Chen Zeng, Qiaoxian Zheng, and Guofu Zhou. Probabilistic skyline queries on uncertain time series. *Neurocomputing*, 191:224–237, 2016. DOI: 10.1016/j.neucom.2015.12.104 60

Katja Hose. Processing skyline queries in p2p systems. In *VLDB Ph.D. Workshop*, pages 36–40, 2005. https://www.academia.edu/4053292/Processing_Skyline_Queries_in_P2P_Systems 27

Katja Hose and Akrivi Vlachou. A survey of skyline processing in highly distributed environments. *The VLDB Journal*, 21(3):359–384, 2011. DOI: 10.1007/s00778-011-0246-6 6, 27

Jiafeng Hua, Hui Zhu, Fengwei Wang, Ximeng Liu, Rongxing Lu, Hao Li, and Yeping Zhang. CINEMA: Efficient and privacy-preserving online medical primary diagnosis with skyline query. *IEEE Internet of Things Journal*, 6(2):1450–1461, 2019. DOI: 10.1109/jiot.2018.2834156 101

Zhenhua Huang, Yang Xiang, Bo Zhang, and Xiaoling Liu. A clustering based approach for skyline diversity. *Expert Systems with Applications*, 38(7):7984–7993, 2011. DOI: 10.1016/j.eswa.2010.12.104 60

Zhiyong Huang, Christian S. Jensen, Hua Lu, and Beng Chin Ooi. Skyline queries against mobile lightweight devices in MANETs. In *Proc. of the 22nd IEEE International Conference on Data Engineering (ICDE)*, page 66, 2006a. DOI: 10.1109/icde.2006.142 27

Zhiyong Huang, Hua Lu, Beng Chin Ooi, and Anthony K. H. Tung. Continuous skyline queries for moving objects. *IEEE Transactions on Knowledge and Data Engineering*, 18(12):1645–1658, 2006b. DOI: 10.1109/tkde.2006.185 32, 55

Daniel P. Huttenlocher, Gregory A. Klanderman, and William Rucklidge. Comparing images using the Hausdorff distance. *IEEE Transactions on Pattern Analysis and Machine Intelligence*, 15(9):850–863, 1993. DOI: 10.1109/34.232073 51

Ihab F. Ilyas, George Beskales, and Mohamed A. Soliman. A survey of top-*k* query processing techniques in relational database systems. *ACM Computing Surveys*, 40(4), 2008. DOI: 10.1145/1391729.1391730 2

Md. Saiful Islam, Rui Zhou, and Chengfei Liu. On answering why-not questions in reverse skyline queries. In *Proc. of the 29th IEEE International Conference on Data Engineering (ICDE)*, pages 973–984, 2013. DOI: 10.1109/icde.2013.6544890 61

Bin Jiang and Jian Pei. Online interval skyline queries on time series. In *Proc. of the 25th IEEE International Conference on Data Engineering (ICDE)*, pages 1036–1047, 2009. DOI: 10.1109/icde.2009.70 60

Bin Jiang, Jian Pei, Xuemin Lin, and Yidong Yuan. Probabilistic skylines on uncertain data: Model and bounding-pruning-refining methods. *Journal of Intelligent Information Systems*, 38(1):1–39, 2012. DOI: 10.1007/s10844-010-0141-4 60

Tao Jiang, Yunjun Gao, Bin Zhang, Dan Lin, and Qing Li. Monochromatic and bichromatic mutual skyline queries. *Expert Systems with Applications*, 41(4):1885–1900, 2014. DOI: 10.1016/j.eswa.2013.08.085 60

Tao Jiang, Bin Zhang, Dan Lin, Yunjun Gao, and Qing Li. Incremental evaluation of top-*k* combinatorial metric skyline query. *Knowledge-Based Systems*, 74:89–105, 2015. DOI: 10.1016/j.knosys.2014.11.009 54

Wen Jin, Jiawei Han, and Martin Ester. Mining thick skylines over large databases. In *Proc. of the 8th European Conference on Principles and Practice of Knowledge Discovery in Databases (PKDD)*, pages 255–266, 2004. DOI: 10.1007/978-3-540-30116-5_25 61

Wen Jin, Michael D. Morse, Jignesh M. Patel, Martin Ester, and Zengjian Hu. Evaluating skylines in the presence of equijoins. In *Proc. of the 26th IEEE International Conference on Data Engineering (ICDE)*, pages 249–260, 2010. DOI: 10.1109/icde.2010.5447841 60

Christos Kalyvas and Theodoros Tzouramanis. A survey of skyline query processing. *CoRR*, 2017. http://arxiv.org/abs/1704.01788 6

Christos Kalyvas, Theodoros Tzouramanis, and Yannis Manolopoulos. Processing skyline queries in temporal databases. In *Proc. of the ACM Symposium on Applied Computing (SAC)*, pages 893–899, 2017. DOI: 10.1145/3019612.3019677 60

Ismail Kertiou, Saber Benharzallah, Laïd Kahloul, Mounir Beggas, Reinhardt Euler, Abdelkader Laouid, and Ahcène Bounceur. A dynamic skyline technique for a context-aware selection of the best sensors in an IoT architecture. *Ad Hoc Networks*, 81:183–196, 2018. DOI: 10.1016/j.adhoc.2018.08.011 106

Mohamed E. Khalefa, Mohamed F. Mokbel, and Justin J. Levandoski. PrefJoin: An efficient preference-aware join operator. In *Proc. of the 27th IEEE International Conference on Data Engineering (ICDE)*, pages 995–1006, 2011. DOI: 10.1109/icde.2011.5767894 60

Kazuki Kodama, Yuichi Iijima, Xi Guo, and Yoshiharu Ishikawa. Skyline queries based on user locations and preferences for making location-based recommendations. In *Proc. of the SIGSPATIAL International Workshop on Location Based Social Networks (LBSN)*, pages 9–16, 2009. DOI: 10.1145/1629890.1629893 48

Henning Köhler, Jing Yang, and Xiaofang Zhou. Efficient parallel skyline processing using hyperplane projections. In *Proc. of the ACM International Conference on Management of Data (SIGMOD)*, pages 85–96, 2011. DOI: 10.1145/1989323.1989333 60

Athanasios Kokkos, Theodoros Tzouramanis, and Yannis Manolopoulos. A hybrid model for linking multiple social identities across heterogeneous online social networks. In *Proc. of the 43rd International Conference on Current Trends in Theory and Practice of Computer Science (SOFSEM)*, pages 423–435, 2017. DOI: 10.1007/978-3-319-51963-0_33 52

Vladlen Koltun and Christos H. Papadimitriou. Approximately dominating representatives. *Theoretical Computer Science*, 371(3):148–154, 2007. DOI: 10.1016/j.tcs.2006.11.003 60

Maria Kontaki, Apostolos N. Papadopoulos, and Yannis Manolopoulos. Continuous k-dominant skyline computation on multidimensional data streams. In *Proc. of the ACM Symposium on Applied Computing (SAC)*, pages 956–960, 2008. DOI: 10.1145/1363686.1363908 39

Maria Kontaki, Apostolos N. Papadopoulos, and Yannis Manolopoulos. Continuous top-k dominating queries. *IEEE Transactions on Knowledge and Data Engineering*, 24(5):840–853, 2012. DOI: 10.1109/TKDE.2011.43 89

Donald Kossmann, Frank Ramsak, and Steffen Rost. Shooting stars in the sky: An online algorithm for skyline queries. In *Proc. of the 28th International Conference on Very Large Data Bases (VLDB)*, pages 275–286, 2002. http://www.vldb.org/conf/2002/S09P01.pdf 22, 23

H. T. Kung, Fabrizio Luccio, and Franco P. Preparata. On finding the maxima of a set of vectors. *Journal of the ACM*, 22(4):469–476, 1975. DOI: 10.1145/321906.321910 6, 13, 17

Chuan-Chi Lai, Zulhaydar Fairozal Akbar, and Chuan-Ming Liu. A cooperative method for processing range-skyline queries in mobile wireless sensor networks. In *Proc. of the 6th International Conference on Emerging Databases: Technologies, Applications and Theory (EDB)*, pages 1–8, 2016. DOI: 10.1145/3007818.3007820 55

Chuan-Chi Lai, Zulhaydar Fairozal Akbar, Chuan-Ming Liu, Van-Dai Ta, and Li-Chun Wang. Distributed continuous range-skyline query monitoring over the internet of mobile things. *IEEE Internet of Things Journal*, 6(4):6652–6667, 2019a. DOI: 10.1109/jiot.2019.2909393 55

Chuan-Chi Lai, Tien-Chun Wang, Chuan-Ming Liu, and Li-Chun Wang. Probabilistic top-k dominating query monitoring over multiple uncertain IoT data streams in edge computing environments. *IEEE Internet of Things Journal*, 6(5):8563–8576, 2019b. DOI: 10.1109/jiot.2019.2920908 90

Iosif Lazaridis and Sharad Mehrotra. Progressive approximate aggregate queries with a multi-resolution tree structure. In *Proc. of the ACM International Conference on Management of Data (SIGMOD)*, pages 401–412, 2001. DOI: 10.1145/375663.375718 67

Jongwuk Lee and Seung-won Hwang. QSkycube: Efficient skycube computation using point-based space partitioning. *Proc. of the VLDB Endowment*, 4(3):185–196, 2010. http://www.vldb.org/pvldb/vol4/p185-lee.pdf DOI: 10.14778/1929861.1929865 41

Jongwuk Lee, Gae-won You, and Seung-won Hwang. Personalized top-k skyline queries in high-dimensional space. *Information Systems*, 34(1):45–61, 2009. DOI: 10.1016/j.is.2008.04.004 61

Ken C. K. Lee, Wang-Chien Lee, Baihua Zheng, Huajing Li, and Yuan Tian. Z-SKY: An efficient skyline query processing framework based on Z-order. *The VLDB Journal*, 19(3):333–362, 2010. DOI: 10.1007/s00778-009-0166-x 39

Justin J. Levandoski, Mohamed F. Mokbel, Mohamed E. Khalefa, and Venkateshwar R. Korukanti. A demonstration of FlexPref: Extensible preference evaluation inside the DBMS engine. In *Proc. of the ACM SIGMOD International Conference on Management of Data*, pages 1247–1250, Association for Computing Machinery New York, 2010. DOI: 10.1145/1807167.1807331 109, 110

Cuiping Li, Beng Chin Ooi, Anthony K. H. Tung, and Shan Wang. DADA: A data cube for dominant relationship analysis. In *Proc. of the ACM International Conference on Management of Data (SIGMOD)*, pages 659–670, 2006a. DOI: 10.1145/1142473.1142547 100

Huajing Li, Qingzhao Tan, and Wang-Chien Lee. Efficient progressive processing of skyline queries in peer-to-peer systems. In *Proc. of the 1st International Conference on Scalable Information Systems (Infoscale)*, pages 26–es, 2006b. DOI: 10.1145/1146847.1146873 27

Jianzhong Li and Shuguang Xiong. Efficient Pr-Skyline query processing and optimization in wireless sensor networks. *Wireless Sensor Network*, 2(11):838–849, 2010. DOI: 10.4236/wsn.2010.211101 28

Rong-Hua Li, Lu Qin, Fanghua Ye, Jeffrey Xu Yu, Xiaokui Xiao, Nong Xiao, and Zibin Zheng. Skyline community search in multi-valued networks. In *Proc. of the International Conference on Management of Data (SIGMOD)*, pages 457–472, 2018. DOI: 10.1145/3183713.3183736 98

Xiang Lian and Lei Chen. Monochromatic and bichromatic reverse skyline search over uncertain databases. In *Proc. of the ACM International Conference on Management of Data (SIGMOD)*, pages 213–226, 2008a. DOI: 10.1145/1376616.1376641 60

Xiang Lian and Lei Chen. Reverse skyline search in uncertain databases. *ACM Transactions on Database Systems*, 35(1):1–49, 2008b. DOI: 10.1145/1670243.1670246 60

Xinmei Liang, Qin Lu, and Mingyu Li. Research on web service selection based on improved skyline algorithm. In *Proc. of the IEEE International Conference on Parallel and Distributed Processing with Applications, Big Data and Cloud Computing, Sustainable Computing and Communications, Social Computing and Networking (ISPA/BDCloud/SocialCom/SustainCom)*, pages 1323–1328, 2019. DOI: 10.1109/ISPA-BDCloud-SustainCom-SocialCom48970.2019.00190 92

Jongtae Lim, Kyoungsoo Bok, and Jaesoo Yoo. A continuous reverse skyline query processing scheme for multimedia data sharing in mobile environments. *Multimedia Tools and Applications*, 78(20):28357–28373, 2019. DOI: 10.1007/s11042-017-5191-y 60

J. G. Lin. Maximal vectors and multi-objective optimization. *Journal of Optimization Theory and Applications*, 18:41–64, 1976. DOI: 10.1007/bf00933793 6

Xin Lin, Jianliang Xu, and Haibo Hu. Range-based skyline queries in mobile environments. *IEEE Transactions on Knowledge and Data Engineering*, 25(4):835–849, 2013. DOI: 10.1109/tkde.2011.229 56

Xuemin Lin, Yidong Yuan, Wei Wang, and Hongjun Lu. Stabbing the sky: Efficient skyline computation over sliding windows. In *Proc. of the 21st IEEE International Conference on Data Engineering (ICDE)*, pages 502–513, 2005. DOI: 10.1109/icde.2005.137 32, 60

Xuemin Lin, Yidong Yuan, Qing Zhang, and Ying Zhang. Selecting stars: The *k* most representative skyline operator. In *Proc. of the 23rd IEEE International Conference on Data Engineering (ICDE)*, pages 86–95, 2007. DOI: 10.1109/icde.2007.367854 60

Jinfei Liu, Li Xiong, Jian Pei, Jun Luo, and Haoyu Zhang. Finding Pareto optimal groups: Group-based skyline. *Proc. of the VLDB Endowment*, 8(13):2086–2097, 2015. DOI: 10.14778/2831360.2831363 60

Xingjie Liu, De-Nian Yang, Mao Ye, and Wang-Chien Lee. U-skyline: A new skyline query for uncertain databases. *IEEE Transactions on Knowledge and Data Engineering*, 25(4):945–960, 2012. DOI: 10.1109/tkde.2012.33 61

Eric Lo, Kevin Y. Yip, King-Ip Lin, and David W. Cheung. Progressive skylining over web-accessible databases. *Data and Knowledge Engineering*, 57(2):122–147, 2006. DOI: 10.1016/j.datak.2005.04.003 20, 27

Christoph Lofi, Ulrich Güntzer, and Wolf-Tilo Balke. Efficient computation of trade-off skylines. In *Proc. of the 13th International Conference on Extending Database Technology (EDBT)*, pages 597–608, 2010. DOI: 10.1145/1739041.1739112 60

Hai-Xin Lu, Yi Luo, and Xuemin Lin. An optimal divide-conquer algorithm for 2D skyline queries. In *Proc. of the 7th East European Conference on Advances in Databases and Information Systems (ADBIS)*, pages 46–60, 2003. DOI: 10.1007/978-3-540-39403-7_6 18

Ming-Hay Luk, Man Lung Yiu, and Eric Lo. Group-by skyline query processing in relational engines. In *Proc. of the 18th ACM Conference on Information and Knowledge Management (CIKM)*, pages 1433–1436, 2009. DOI: 10.1145/1645953.1646138 60

Yi Luo, Hai-Xin Lu, and Xuemin Lin. A scalable and I/O optimal skyline processing algorithm. In *Proc. of the 5th International Conference on Advances in Web-Age Information Management (WAIM)*, pages 218–228, 2004. DOI: 10.1007/978-3-540-27772-9_23 26

Zhixin Ma, Kai Zhang, Shaoliang Wang, and Chaojie Yu. A double-index-based k-dominant skyline algorithm for incomplete data stream. In *Proc. of the 4th IEEE International Conference on Software Engineering and Service Science (ICSESS)*, pages 750–753, 2013. DOI: 10.1109/icsess.2013.6615414 40

Matteo Magnani and Ira Assent. From stars to galaxies: Skyline queries on aggregate data. In *Proc. of the Joint EDBT/ICDT Conferences*, pages 477–488, 2013. DOI: 10.1145/2452376.2452432 60

Yannis Manolopoulos, Alexandros Nanopoulos, Apostolos N. Papadopoulos, and Yannis Theodoridis. R-Trees: Theory and applications. *Advanced Information and Knowledge Processing*, Springer, 2006. DOI: 10.1007/978-1-84628-293-5 22

Xiaoye Miao, Yunjun Gao, Gang Chen, and Tianyi Zhang. k-dominant skyline queries on incomplete data. *Information Sciences*, 367–368:990–1011, 2016. DOI: 10.1016/j.ins.2016.07.034 40

Xiaoye Miao, Yunjun Gao, Su Guo, and Gang Chen. On efficiently answering why-not range-based skyline queries in road networks. *IEEE Transactions on Knowledge and Data Engineering*, 30(9):1697–1711, 2018. DOI: 10.1109/TKDE.2018.2803821 61

Denis Mindolin and Jan Chomicki. Preference elicitation in prioritized skyline queries. *The VLDB Journal*, 20(2):157–182, 2011. DOI: 10.1007/s00778-011-0227-9 60

Michael D. Morse, Jignesh M. Patel, and William I. Grosky. Efficient continuous skyline computation. *Information Sciences*, 177(17):3411–3437, 2007a. 32

Michael D. Morse, Jignesh M. Patel, and H. V. Jagadish. Efficient skyline computation over low-cardinality domains. In *Proc. of the 33rd International Conference on Very Large Data Bases (VLDB)*, pages 267–278, 2007b. http://www.vldb.org/conf/2007/papers/research/p267-morse.pdf 60

Dimitris Papadias, Panos Kalnis, Jun Zhang, and Yufei Tao. Efficient OLAP operations in spatial data warehouses. In *Proc. of the 7th International Symposium on Advances in Spatial and Temporal Databases (SSTD)*, pages 443–459, 2001. DOI: 10.1007/3-540-47724-1_23 67, 73

Dimitris Papadias, Yufei Tao, Greg Fu, and Bernhard Seeger. An optimal and progressive algorithm for skyline queries. In *Proc. of the ACM International Conference on Management of Data (SIGMOD)*, pages 467–478, 2003. DOI: 10.1145/872757.872814 23, 26, 43, 44, 52, 54, 60

Dimitris Papadias, Yufei Tao, Greg Fu, and Bernhard Seeger. Progressive skyline computation in database systems. *ACM Transactions on Database Systems*, 30(1):41–82, 2005a. DOI: 10.1145/1061318.1061320 30, 64, 66, 73, 85

Dimitris Papadias, Yufei Tao, Kyriakos Mouratidis, and Chun Kit Hui. Aggregate nearest neighbor queries in spatial databases. *ACM Transactions Database Systems*, 30(2):529–576, 2005b. DOI: 10.1145/1071610.1071616 86, 87

Jian Pei, Wen Jin, Martin Ester, and Yufei Tao. Catching the best views of skyline: A semantic approach based on decisive subspaces. In *Proc. of the 31st International Conference on Very Large Data Bases (VLDB)*, pages 253–264, 2005. http://www.vldb.org/archives/website/2005/program/paper/tue/p253-pei.pdf 41

Yi-Wen Peng and Wei-Mei Chen. Parallel *k*-dominant skyline queries in high-dimensional datasets. *Information Sciences*, 496:538–552, 2019. DOI: 10.1016/j.ins.2019.01.039 40

Franco P. Preparata and Michael I. Shamos. *Computational Geometry: An Introduction*. Texts and Monographs in Computer Science, Springer, Berlin, Heidelberg, 1985. DOI: 10.1007/978-1-4612-1098-6 6, 17

Venkatesh Raghavan, Elke A. Rundensteiner, and Shweta Srivastava. Skyline and mapping aware join query evaluation. *Information Systems*, 36(6):917–936, 2011. DOI: 10.1016/j.is.2011.03.002 60

Md Farhadur Rahman, Abolfazl Asudeh, Nick Koudas, and Gautam Das. Efficient computation of subspace skyline over categorical domains. In *Proc. of the ACM International Conference on Information and Knowledge Management (CIKM)*, pages 407–416, 2017. DOI: 10.1145/3132847.3133012 60

Saladi Rahul and Ravi Janardan. Algorithms for range-skyline queries. In *Proc. of the 20th ACM International Conference on Advances in Geographic Information Systems (SIGSPATIAL)*, pages 526–529, 2012. DOI: 10.1145/2424321.2424406 xvii, 56

Chedy Raïssi, Jian Pei, and Thomas Kister. Computing closed skycubes. *Proc. of the VLDB Endowment*, 3(1):838–847, 2010. http://www.vldb.org/pvldb/vldb2010/pvldb_vol3/R75.pdf DOI: 10.14778/1920841.1920948 42

Dimitris Sacharidis, Panagiotis Bouros, and Timos K. Sellis. Caching dynamic skyline queries. In *Proc. of the 20th International Conference on Scientific and Statistical Database Management (SSDBM)*, pages 455–472, 2008. DOI: 10.1007/978-3-540-69497-7_29 44

Dimitris Sacharidis, Stavros Papadopoulos, and Dimitris Papadias. Topologically sorted skylines for partially ordered domains. In *Proc. of the 25th IEEE International Conference on Data Engineering (ICDE)*, pages 1072–1083, 2009. DOI: 10.1109/icde.2009.129 60

Maytham Safar, Dalal El-Amin, and David Taniar. Optimized skyline queries on road networks using nearest neighbors. *Personal and Ubiquitous Computing*, 15(8):845–856, 2011. DOI: 10.1007/s00779-011-0371-7 47

Fayçal Rédha Saidani, Allel Hadjali, Idir Rassoul, and Djamal Belkasmi. Skyline-based feature selection for polarity classification in social networks. In *Proc. of the 28th International Conference on Database and Expert Systems Applications (DEXA)*, I:381–394, 2017. DOI: 10.1007/978-3-319-64468-4_29 94

Chaluka Salgado. Keyword-aware skyline routes search in indoor venues. In *Proc. of the 9th ACM SIGSPATIAL International Workshop on Indoor Spatial Awareness (ISA)*, pages 25–31, 2018. DOI: 10.1145/3282461.3282467 108, 109

Nikos Sarkas, Gautam Das, Nick Koudas, and Anthony K. H. Tung. Categorical skylines for streaming data. In *Proc. of the ACM International Conference on Management of Data (SIGMOD)*, pages 239–250, 2008. DOI: 10.1145/1376616.1376643 60

Atish Das Sarma, Ashwin Lall, Danupon Nanongkai, Richard J. Lipton, and Jun (Jim) Xu. Representative skylines using threshold-based preference distributions. In *Proc. of the 27th IEEE International Conference on Data Engineering (ICDE)*, pages 387–398, 2011. DOI: 10.1109/icde.2011.5767873 60

Mehdi Sharifzadeh and Cyrus Shahabi. The spatial skyline queries. In *Proc. of the 32nd International Conference on Very Large Data Bases (VLDB)*, pages 751–762, 2006. http://dl.acm.org/citation.cfm?id=1164192 46

Bojie Shen, Saiful Islam, and David Taniar. Direction-based spatial skyline for retrieving arbitrary-shaped surrounding objects. *The Computer Journal*, 2019. DOI: 10.1093/comjnl/bxz099 51

Bojie Shen, Saiful Islam, David Taniar, and Junhu Wang. Direction-based spatial skyline for retrieving surrounding objects. *World Wide Web*, 23(1):207–239, 2020. DOI: 10.1007/s11280-019-00694-w 50

Jieming Shi, Dingming Wu, and Nikos Mamoulis. Textually relevant spatial skylines. *IEEE Transactions on Knowledge and Data Engineering*, 28(1):224–237, 2015. DOI: 10.1109/tkde.2015.2465374 49

Mohammad Anisuzzaman Siddique, Hao Tian, and Yasuhiko Morimoto. *k*-dominant skyline query computation in MapReduce environment. *IEICE TRANSACTIONS on Information and Systems*, 98-D(5):1027–1034, 2015. DOI: 10.1587/transinf.2014DAP0010 40

Mohammad Anisuzzaman Siddique, Hao Tian, Mahboob Qaosar, and Yasuhiko Morimoto. MapReduce algorithm for variants of skyline queries: Skyband and dominating queries. *Algorithms*, 12(8), 2019. DOI: 10.3390/a12080166 90

Antonis Sidiropoulos, Antonia Gogoglou, Dimitrios Katsaros, and Yannis Manolopoulos. Gazing at the skyline for star scientists. *Journal of Informetrics*, 10(3):789–813, 2016. DOI: 10.1016/j.joi.2016.04.009 105

Tomás Skopal. Pivoting M-tree: A metric access method for efficient similarity search. In *Proc. of the Annual International Workshop on DAtabases, TExts, Specifications and Objects (DATESO)*, pages 27–37, 2004. http://ceur-ws.org/Vol-98/paper3.pdf 52, 53

Tomás Skopal and Jakub Lokoc. Answering metric skyline queries by PM-tree. In *Proc. of the Annual International Workshop on DAtabases, TExts, Specifications and Objects (DATESO)*, pages 22–37, 2010. http://ceur-ws.org/Vol-567/paper03.pdf 53

Wanbin Son, Mu-Woong Lee, Hee-Kap Ahn, and Seung-won Hwang. Spatial skyline queries: An efficient geometric algorithm. In *Proc. of the 11th International Symposium on Spatial and Temporal Databases (SSTD)*, pages 247–264, 2009. DOI: 10.1007/978-3-642-02982-0_17 47

Wanbin Son, Seung-won Hwang, and Hee-Kap Ahn. MSSQ: Manhattan spatial skyline queries. *Information Systems*, 40:67–83, 2014. DOI: 10.1016/j.is.2013.10.001 47

Georgios Stoupas, Antonis Sidiropoulos, Antonia Gogoglou, Dimitrios Katsaros, and Yannis Manolopoulos. Rainbow ranking: an adaptable, multidimensional ranking method for publication sets. *Scientometrics*, 116(1):147–160, 2018. DOI: 10.1007/s11192-018-2731-9 106

Ping Sun, Caimei Liang, Guohui Li, and Ling Yuan. Researching why-not questions in skyline query based on orthogonal range. *Electronics*, 9(3):500, 2020. DOI: 10.3390/electronics9030500 61

Kian-Lee Tan, Pin-Kwang Eng, and Beng Chin Ooi. Efficient progressive skyline computation. In *Proc. of the 27th International Conference on Very Large Data Bases (VLDB)*, pages 301–310, 2001. http://www.vldb.org/conf/2001/P301.pdf 18, 20

Bo Tang, Kyriakos Mouratidis, Man Lung Yiu, and Zhenyu Chen. Creating top ranking options in the continuous option and preference space. *Proc. of the VLDB Endowment*, 12(10):1181–1194, 2019. DOI: 10.14778/3339490.3339500 99

Yufei Tao. Diversity in skylines. *IEEE Data Engineering Bulletin*, 32(4):65–72, 2009. http://sites.computer.org/debull/A09dec/yufei-paper.pdf 34

Yufei Tao and Dimitris Papadias. Maintaining sliding window skylines on data streams. *IEEE Transactions on Knowledge and Data Engineering*, 18(3):377–391, 2006. DOI: 10.1109/tkde.2006.48 32

Yufei Tao, Xiaokui Xiao, and Jian Pei. SUBSKY: Efficient computation of skylines in subspaces. In *Proc. of the 22nd IEEE International Conference on Data Engineering (ICDE)*, page 65, 2006. DOI: 10.1109/icde.2006.149 34

Yufei Tao, Ling Ding, Xuemin Lin, and Jian Pei. Distance-based representative skyline. In *Proc. of the 25th IEEE International Conference on Data Engineering (ICDE)*, pages 892–903, 2009. DOI: 10.1109/icde.2009.84 60

Nilu Thakur. Skyline queries. In Shashi Shekhar, Hui Xiong, and Xun Zhou, Eds., *Encyclopedia of GIS*, pages 1897–1905, Springer, 2017. DOI: 10.1007/978-3-319-23519-6_1221-2 6

Eleftherios Tiakas, Apostolos N. Papadopoulos, and Yannis Manolopoulos. Progressive processing of subspace dominating queries. *The VLDB Journal*, 20(6):921–948, 2011. DOI: 10.1007/s00778-011-0231-0 74, 82, 83

Eleftherios Tiakas, Apostolos N. Papadopoulos, and Yannis Manolopoulos. On estimating the maximum domination value and the skyline cardinality of multi-dimensional data sets. *International Journal of Knowledge-based Organizations*, 3(4):61–83, 2013. DOI: 10.4018/ijkbo.2013100104 33, 69

Eleftherios Tiakas, George Valkanas, Apostolos N. Papadopoulos, and Yannis Manolopoulos. Metric-based top-k dominating queries. In *Proc. of the 17th International Conference on Extending Database Technology (EDBT)*, pages 415–426, 2014. DOI: 10.5441/002/edbt.2014.38 83, 84, 88, 89

Eleftherios Tiakas, Apostolos N. Papadopoulos, and Yannis Manolopoulos. Skyline queries: An introduction. In *Proc. of the 6th International Conference on Information, Intelligence, Systems and Applications (IISA)*, pages 1–6, 2015. DOI: 10.1109/iisa.2015.7388053 6

Eleftherios Tiakas, George Valkanas, Apostolos N. Papadopoulos, Yannis Manolopoulos, and Dimitrios Gunopulos. Processing top-k dominating queries in metric spaces. *ACM Transactions on Database Systems*, 40(4), 2016. DOI: 10.1145/2847524 83, 84, 88, 89

Theodoros Tzouramanis, Eleftherios Tiakas, Apostolos N. Papadopoulos, and Yannis Manolopoulos. The range skyline query. In *Proc. of the 27th ACM International Conference on Information and Knowledge Management (CIKM)*, pages 47–56, 2018. DOI: 10.1145/3269206.3271693 58

George Valkanas, Apostolos N. Papadopoulos, and Dimitrios Gunopulos. SkyDiver: A framework for skyline diversification. In *Proc. of the Joint EDBT/ICDT Conferences*, pages 406–417, 2013. DOI: 10.1145/2452376.2452424 34

George Valkanas, Apostolos N. Papadopoulos, and Dimitrios Gunopulos. Skyline ranking à la IR. In *Proc. of the Workshops of the EDBT/ICDT Joint Conference*, pages 182–187, 2014. http://ceur-ws.org/Vol-1133/paper-31.pdf 34

Akrivi Vlachou, Christos Doulkeridis, Yannis Kotidis, and Michalis Vazirgiannis. SKYPEER: Efficient subspace skyline computation over distributed data. In *Proc. of the 23rd IEEE International Conference on Data Engineering (ICDE)*, pages 416–425, 2007. DOI: 10.1109/icde.2007.367887 27

Akrivi Vlachou, Christos Doulkeridis, and Yannis Kotidis. Angle-based space partitioning for efficient parallel skyline computation. In *Proc. of the ACM International Conference on Management of Data (SIGMOD)*, pages 227–238, 2008. DOI: 10.1145/1376616.1376642 28, 30

Akrivi Vlachou, Christos Doulkeridis, Yannis Kotidis, and Michalis Vazirgiannis. Efficient routing of subspace skyline queries over highly distributed data. *IEEE Transactions on Knowledge and Data Engineering*, 22(12):1694–1708, 2010. DOI: 10.1109/tkde.2009.204 27

Akrivi Vlachou, Christos Doulkeridis, and Neoklis Polyzotis. Skyline query processing over joins. In *Proc. of the ACM International Conference on Management of Data (SIGMOD)*, pages 73–84, 2011. DOI: 10.1145/1989323.1989332 60

Changping Wang, Chaokun Wang, Gaoyang Guo, Xiaojun Ye, and S. Yu Philip. Efficient computation of G-skyline groups. *IEEE Transactions on Knowledge and Data Engineering*, 30(4):674–688, 2017a. DOI: 10.1109/TKDE.2017.2777994 60

Guoren Wang, Junchang Xin, Lei Chen, and Yunhao Liu. Energy-efficient reverse skyline query processing over wireless sensor networks. *IEEE Transactions on Knowledge and Data Engineering*, 24(7):1259–1275, 2011a. DOI: 10.1109/tkde.2011.64 60

Hongbing Wang, Xingguo Hu, Qi Yu, Mingzhu Gu, Wei Zhao, Jia Yan, and Tianjing Hong. Integrating reinforcement learning and skyline computing for adaptive service composition. *Information Sciences*, 519:141–160, 2020a. DOI: 10.1016/j.ins.2020.01.039 91

Shiqing Wang, Yuanyuan Li, Zhiyang Li, Junfeng Wu, and Fengjuan Chen. Surveillance methods of running condition of chemical equipments based on skyline. In *Proc. of the IEEE Trustcom/BigDataSE/ISPA Joint Conferences*, pages 2246–2250, 2016a. DOI: 10.1109/trustcom.2016.0346 106

Shiyuan Wang, Beng Chin Ooi, Anthony K. H. Tung, and Lizhen Xu. Efficient skyline query processing on peer-to-peer networks. In *Proc. of the 23rd IEEE International Conference on Data Engineering (ICDE)*, pages 1126–1135, 2007. DOI: 10.1109/icde.2007.368971 27

Shiyuan Wang, Quang Hieu Vu, Beng Chin Ooi, Anthony K. H. Tung, and Lizhen Xu. Skyframe: A framework for skyline query processing in peer-to-peer systems. *The VLDB Journal*, 18(1):345–362, 2009. DOI: 10.1007/s00778-008-0104-3 27

Weiguo Wang, Hui Li, Yanguo Peng, Sourav S. Bhowmick, Peng Chen, Xiaofeng Chen, and Jiangtao Cui. An efficient secure dynamic skyline query model. *CoRR*, 2020b. https://arxiv.org/abs/2002.07511 45

Wen-Chi Wang, En Tzu Wang, and Arbee L. P. Chen. Dynamic skylines considering range queries. In *Proc. of the 16th International Conference on Database Systems for Advanced Applications (DASFAA)*, II:235–250, 2011b. DOI: 10.1007/978-3-642-20152-3_18 57, 58

Wenlu Wang, Ji Zhang, Min-Te Sun, and Wei-Shinn Ku. Efficient parallel spatial skyline evaluation using MapReduce. In *Proc. of the 20th International Conference on Extending Database Technology (EDBT)*, pages 426–437, 2017b. DOI: 10.5441/002/edbt.2017.38 51

Zonghui Wang, Yunjun Gao, Qing Liu, Xiaoye Miao, Qing Li, and Chuan Li. Efficient group-by reverse skyline computation. *World Wide Web*, 19(6):1023–1049, 2016b. DOI: 10.1007/s11280-015-0372-y 60

Ping Wu, Caijie Zhang, Ying Feng, Ben Y. Zhao, Divyakant Agrawal, and Amr El Abbadi. Parallelizing skyline queries for scalable distribution. In *Proc. of the 10th International Conference on Extending Database Technology (EDBT)*, pages 112–130, 2006. DOI: 10.1007/11687238_10 27

Tian Xia, Donghui Zhang, Zheng Fang, Cindy Chen, and Jie Wang. Online subspace skyline query processing using the compressed skycube. *ACM Transactions on Database Systems*, 37(2), 2012. DOI: 10.1145/2188349.2188357 34, 42

Xike Xie, Hua Lu, Jinchuan Chen, and Shuo Shang. Top-*k* neighborhood dominating query. In *Proc. of the 18th International Conference on Database Systems for Advanced Applications (DAS-FAA)*, pages 131–145, 2013. DOI: 10.1007/978-3-642-37487-6_12 89

Wei Xiong, Zhao Wu, Bing Li, and Bo Hang. Reliability ranking prediction for cloud services via skyline. In *Proc. of the 5th IEEE International Conference on Cyber Security and Cloud Computing (CSCloud), 4th IEEE International Conference on Edge Computing and Scalable Cloud (EdgeCom)*, pages 64–74, 2018. DOI: 10.1109/cscloud/edgecom.2018.00021 93

Fadoua Yakine, Manar Abourezq, and Abdellah Idrissi. Skyline method in wireless ad-hoc networks routing. *WSEAS Transactions on Communications*, 15:137–146, 2016. http://www.wseas.org/multimedia/journals/communications/2016/a345804-898.pdf 106

Bo Yin, Xuetao Wei, and Yonghe Liu. Finding the informative and concise set through approximate skyline queries. *Expert Systems with Applications*, 119:289–310, 2019. DOI: 10.1016/j.eswa.2018.11.004 60

Bo Yin, Xuetao Wei, Jin Wang, Naixue Xiong, and Ke Gu. An industrial dynamic skyline based similarity joins for multi-dimensional big data applications. *IEEE Transactions on Industrial Informatics*, 16(4):2520–2532, 2020. DOI: 10.1109/tii.2019.2933534 60

Man Lung Yiu and Nikos Mamoulis. Efficient processing of top-*k* dominating queries on multi-dimensional data. In *Proc. of the 33rd International Conference on Very Large Data Bases (VLDB)*, pages 483–494, 2007. http://www.vldb.org/conf/2007/papers/research/p483-yiu.pdf 66, 67, 68, 69, 71, 73

Man Lung Yiu and Nikos Mamoulis. Multi-dimensional top-*k* dominating queries. *The VLDB Journal*, 18(3):695–718, 2009. DOI: 10.1007/s00778-008-0117-y 66, 67, 68, 69, 71, 72, 73

Gae-won You, Mu-Woong Lee, Hyeonseung Im, and Seung-won Hwang. The farthest spatial skyline queries. *Information Systems*, 38(3):286–301, 2013. DOI: 10.1016/j.is.2012.10.001 48

Jing Yu, Xin Liu, and Guo-hua Liu. A window-based algorithm for skyline queries. In *Proc. of the 6th International Conference on Parallel and Distributed Computing, Applications and Technologies (PDCAT)*, pages 907–909, 2005. DOI: 10.1109/pdcat.2005.58 32

Yidong Yuan, Xuemin Lin, Qing Liu, Wei Wang, Jeffrey Xu Yu, and Qing Zhang. Efficient computation of the skyline cube. In *Proc. of the 31st International Conference on Very Large Data Bases (VLDB)*, pages 241–252, 2005. http://www.vldb.org/archives/website/2005/program/paper/tue/p241-yuan.pdf 41

Sepanta Zeighami, Gabriel Ghinita, and Cyrus Shahabi. Dynamic skyline queries on encrypted data using result materialization. *CoRR*, 2020. https://arxiv.org/abs/2003.00051 45

Kaiqi Zhang, Hong Gao, Xixian Han, Donghua Yang, Zhipeng Cai, and Jianzhong Li. RSky-cube: Efficient skycube computation by reusing principle. In *Proc. of the 22nd International Conference on Database Systems for Advanced Applications (DASFAA)*, vol. II, 2017. DOI: 10.1007/978-3-319-55699-4_4 41

Shiming Zhang, Nikos Mamoulis, and David W. Cheung. Scalable skyline computation using object-based space partitioning. In *Proc. of the ACM International Conference on Management of Data (SIGMOD)*, pages 483–494, 2009a. DOI: 10.1145/1559845.1559897 39

Wenjie Zhang, Xuemin Lin, Ying Zhang, Wei Wang, and Jeffrey Xu Yu. Probabilistic skyline operator over sliding windows. In *Proc. of the 25th IEEE International Conference on Data Engineering (ICDE)*, pages 1060–1071, 2009b. DOI: 10.1109/ICDE.2009.83 60

Wenjie Zhang, Xuemin Lin, Ying Zhang, and Wei Wang. Threshold-based probabilistic top-k dominating queries. *The VLDB Journal*, 19(4):283–305, 2010a. DOI: 10.1007/s00778-009-0162-1 89

Wenjie Zhang, Xuemin Lin, Ying Zhang, Muhammad Aamir Cheema, and Qing Zhang. Stochastic skylines. *ACM Transactions on Database Systems*, 37(2), 2012. DOI: 10.1145/2188349.2188356 60

Wenjie Zhang, Xuemin Lin, Ying Zhang, Wei Wang, Gaoping Zhu, and Jeffrey Xu Yu. Probabilistic skyline operator over sliding windows. *Information Systems*, 38(8):1212–1233, 2013. DOI: 10.1016/j.is.2012.03.002 60

Zhenjie Zhang, Hua Lu, Beng Chin Ooi, and Anthony K. H. Tung. Understanding the meaning of a shifted sky: A general framework on extending skyline query. *The VLDB Journal*, 19(2):181–201, 2010b. DOI: 10.1007/s00778-009-0148-z 61

Xu Zhou, Kenli Li, ZhiBang Yang, and Keqin Li. Finding optimal skyline product combinations under price promotion. *IEEE Transactions on Knowledge and Data Engineering*, 31(1):138–151, 2019. DOI: 10.1109/tkde.2018.2823707 107

Xu Zhou, Kenli Li, Zhibang Yang, Yunjun Gao, and Keqin Li. Efficient approaches to k representative G-skyline queries. *ACM Transactions on Knowledge Discovery from Data*, 14(5), 2020. DOI: 10.1145/3397503 60

Lei Zou, Lei Chen, M. Tamer Özsu, and Dongyan Zhao. Dynamic skyline queries in large graphs. In *Proc. of the 15th International Conference on Database Systems for Advanced Applications (DASFAA)*, II:62–78, 2010. DOI: 10.1007/978-3-642-12098-5_5 44

Authors' Biographies

APOSTOLOS N. PAPADOPOULOS

Apostolos N. Papadopoulos is an Associate Professor of Computer Science at the School of Informatics of Aristotle University of Thessaloniki (AUTH). He received his five-year Diploma Degree in Computer Engineering and Informatics from the University of Patras, and his Ph.D. Degree in Informatics from the School of Informatics (AUTH). His research interests include Data Management, Data Mining, and Big Data Analytics. He has served as a track co-chair of ACM SAC DTTA (Database Technologies Techniques and Applications) Track from 2005 until now, as well as a PC member in several International Conferences related to Data Management and Data Mining. He has co-presented four tutorials in ASONAM 2015, EDBT/ICDT 2016, ICDM 2016, and ECML/PKDD 2017 on the "Core Decomposition of Networks." The paper "SkyGraph: an algorithm for important subgraph discovery in relational graphs," *Proceedings of ECML/PKDD*, Antwerp, Belgium, 2008, received the Best Knowledge Discovery Paper Award, whereas the paper "Metric-Based Top-k Dominating Queries," Proceedings of the 17th International Conference on Extending Database Technology (EDBT), Athens, 2014, was selected as the best paper for publication in *ACM Transactions on Database Systems*. Based on Google Scholar, he has around 3200 citations in his research work.

ELEFTHERIOS TIAKAS

Eleftherios Tiakas received a B.Sc. in Mathematics (1994), a B.Sc. and an M.Sc. in Informatics (2006), and a Ph.D. in Informatics (2011), all the degrees from the Aristotle University of Thessaloniki (AUTH). During the period 2004–2017, he served as Teacher of Mathematics in Secondary Education. From 2011–2017, he served as Adjunct Lecturer with the School of Informatics of AUTH. Since 2017, he has been on the Laboratory Teaching Staff with the School of Informatics of AUTH. His areas of research interest include: Databases, Data Structures, Data Mining, Information Retrieval, Similarity Search, Social Networks, and Bioinformatics. He is the author/co-author of 30 articles published in international journals and conference proceedings, plus 2 book chapters. His publications have received over 600 citations. He participated in 11 research projects and programs funded by the European Union and Greece. Finally, he serves as a PC member and reviewer for several international journals and conferences.

THEODOROS TZOURAMANIS

Theodoros Tzouramanis is an Assistant Professor in the Department of Computer Science and Biomedical Informatics of the University of Thessaly. He received a five-year Diploma Degree in Electrical and Computer Engineering and a Ph.D. in Informatics, both from the Aristotle University of Thessaloniki. Prior to his current position, he served from 2003–2019 as Lecturer and later as Assistant Professor in the Department of Information and Communication Systems Engineering of the University of the Aegean. He has also been teaching at the Hellenic Open University since 2005. His research interests focus on data management, data security, and privacy. More than 50 articles of his work have appeared in refereed scientific journals, conference proceedings, and chapters in books.

NIKOLAOS GEORGIADIS

Nikolaos Georgiadis is a Ph.D. candidate at the School of Informatics of Aristotle University of Thessaloniki (AUTH). He has a B.Sc. in Software Engineering from the Technical University of Kavala and a M.Sc. in Information Systems from the School of Informatics of AUTH. His main research interests focus on efficient algorithmic techniques for Knowledge Discovery from Big Data. He has professional experience as a Software Engineer in the IT industry in various companies in Greece, Germany, and Switzerland for over 15 years.

YANNIS MANOLOPOULOS

Yannis Manolopoulos is a Professor and Vice-rector of the Open University of Cyprus. He received a five-year Diploma Degree in Electrical Engineering and a Ph.D. in Computer Engineering, both from the Aristotle University of Thessaloniki (AUTH). He has been with the University of Toronto, the University of Maryland at College Park, the University of Cyprus, the Hellenic Open University, and AUTH, where he served as Head of the School of Informatics. He has also served as Rector of the University of Western Macedonia in Greece and Vice-Chair of the Greek Computer Society. His research interest focuses on Data Management. He has co-authored 5 monographs and 11 textbooks in Greek, as well as >300 journal and conference papers. He has received >14,700 citations from >2,200 distinct academic institutions (h-index=57). He has also received 5 best paper awards from SIGMOD, ECML/PKDD, MEDES (2), and ISSPIT conferences and has been invited as keynote speaker at 20 international events. He has served as the main co-organizer of several CORE A/B conferences: SSTD 2003, SSDBM 2004, ADBIS 2006, ICANN 2010, WISE 2013, CAISE 2014, TPDL 2017, DASFAA 2018, IDEAS 2019, WI 2019, and SOFSEM 2020. He has also acted as an evaluator for funding agencies in Austria, Canada, Cyprus, Czech Republic, Estonia, EU, Georgia, Greece, Hong-Kong, Israel, Italy, Lithuania, Poland, and Russia. Currently, he serves on the Editorial Boards of the following journals (among others): *Information Systems*, *World Wide Web*, *Computer Journal*, *Data Science and Analytics*, and *Artificial Intelligence Tools*.

Index

Printed in the United States
by Baker & Taylor Publisher Services